Rick Louis LoBello

Guide to Rwanda's Volcanoes National Park

Home to critically endangered mountain gorillas

Copyright © 2009 by Rick Louis LoBello

© 2009 by Rick Louis LoBello. Revised June, 2014

For guidebook updates and more visit www.iloveparks.com/rwanda

Interact with the author at facebook.com/groups/friendsofgorillas

All rights reserved.

ISBN 1440405190

EAN-13 is 9781440405198

Printed in the United States of America.

No part of this publication may be reproduced, stored in a retrieval system or transmitted in any form or by any means, electronic, mechanical, photocopying, recording, or otherwise without permission of the copyright holder.

Photographers listed in the Photo Credits hold the copyright for their images as noted.

To the people of Rwanda and for the
mountain gorillas of the Virungas

Young Rwandans living near the park boundary gather to watch trackers celebrate their accomplishments at a party sponsored by Partners in Conservation of the Columbus Zoo in Ohio.

They are other nations, caught with ourselves in the net of life and time, fellow prisoners of the splendor and travail of the earth.
                                                        --Henry Beston

Guhonda, 43 year old silverback in the Sabyinyo Group.

Contents

Acknowledgments 1
Introduction 4

Chapters:
1: Land of the Mountain Gorilla 9
2: Planning Your Trip 26
3: Geology of Volcanoes National Park 39
4: The People of Rwanda... 50
5: Dian Fossey 66
6: The Mountain Gorillas 91
7: Plants of Volcanoes National Park 121
8: Birds of of Volcanoes National Park 139
9: Mammals of Volcanoes National Park 156
10: Other Animals of Volcanoes National Park 168
11: Exploring More of the Park and Beyond the Virungas..................................... 177
12: Securing the Park's Future 188

Bibliography 201
Appendix.. 208
Gorilla Conservation Organizations 208
Volcanoes National Park Bird List 211
Volcanoes National Park Mammal List 220
Volcanoes National Park Reptile and Amphibian List... 226
Index 229
Photo Credits 237

Acknowledgments

Over the past 20 years the people of Rwanda have come an incredibly long way in rebuilding their country after the terrible genocide of 1994. As was the case during the 1980s ecotourism is once again becoming an important part of the country's economy and under the leadership of President Paul Kagame, Rwanda may now be one of the safest countries to visit on the African continent. The country truly can be described as a "new Rwanda" and it is my hope that this book will encourage its readers to take an interest in helping Rwandans move towards a brighter future.

I want to thank Clare Richardson, President and CEO of the Dian Fossey Gorilla Fund International (DFGFI) and Dr. Katie Fawcett, past Director of the Karisoke Research Center for all their help in getting this project off the ground. Karisoke Research Center staff members were very helpful whenever I visited the park and I thank all of those who came to my assistance including Fidele Uwimana, Fidele Nsengiyumva, Felix Ndagijimana and John Kalinijabo. I also want to thank the Rwanda Development Board staff (formerly called ORTPN) who kindly assisted me at the park, met with me at my hotel base in Rwanda and responded to my many emails upon my return to the US; Olivier Nzabonimana, Francis Ndagijimana, Fidèle Ruzigandekwe, Pascal Habimana, Alfonse Mwumvaneza and Francis Bayingana.

My good friend and fellow Rotarian Bob Peterson reviewed and edited the manuscript. If it wasn't for Bob helping me move on from one chapter to the next I would have been hard pressed to finish the project. I also want to thank the late Dr. Alecia Lilly, Vice President of Africa Programs for DFGFI and Dr. Tara Stoinski, The Pat and Forest McGrath Chair of Research and Conservation for DFGFI, for their help in reviewing the manuscript. Dr. Stoinski will become President of DFGFI in October, 2014.

During the course of writing this book I was very fortunate to meet Judy Chidester who was a friend of Dian Fossey and spent time at the Karisoke Research Center. Judy had the great fortune of helping to care for an orphan mountain gorilla that Fossey wrote about in her book *Gorillas in the Mist*. I am so very grateful to have met this wonderful lady who not only granted me an interview, but also gave me permission to reprint and include an article she wrote for the U.S. State Department.

The photo credits listed in the Appendix include the names of many individuals who were kind enough to help me assemble the images and graphics I needed to complete this project. I am grateful to them all and want to especially thank Dr. Alan Goodall, Samantha Lloyd, the United Nations Photo Library and the National Geographic Society.

In 2003 when I was considering the possibility of working on a project to help the gorillas and the Dian Fossey Gorilla Fund International, I was able to meet another friend of Dian Fossey, the late Rosamond Carr, author of *Land of a Thousand Hills*. We shared tea in her home when I visited the orphanage she started in Rubavu. When we met I sensed having the unique opportunity of not only meeting one of the greatest ladies Rwanda has ever known, but also someone who shared the commitment and spirit of Dian Fossey, two American women living in Rwanda who gave their lives to something much greater than themselves.

Finally and most importantly I thank my mother the late Shirley LoBello, who as a child inspired me to care about animals and everything life brought my way including the opportunity to write this book.

Rick LoBello, June 1, 2014

Nyakalima, a lone silverback who in 2008 was following the Sabyinyo Group and Group 13.

Introduction

    Volcanoes National Park is a dream ecotourism destination for a growing number of people around the world. In 2005 at the request of the Dian Fossey Gorilla Fund International, the author returned to Rwanda to begin work as a volunteer on the park's first ever guidebook. After spending twenty-five years working at several US National Parks as a park ranger, researcher, educator and park administrator, Rick LoBello was well prepared to take on the task at hand. Working from the Hotel Muhabura and the Karisoke Research Center in Musanze, the guidebook was initially planned with the help of staff at the Karisoke Research Center and at Volcanoes National Park Headquarters at Kinigi. The twelve chapters that follow were written to help provide both important and informative insights for travelers who are planning a trip or are already on their way to visit the park and the gorillas.

The book provides a comprehensive look at Volcanoes National Park including information on how to plan for a trek to see the mountain gorillas, how to watch the gorillas, plus an overview of the region's human and natural history including the story of Dian Fossey. Other points of interest in Rwanda are described in chapter 11.

The Appendix includes a bird list, mammal list and a reptile and amphibian list. For a complete list of plants known to the park, book notes, park updates and more visit www.iloveparks.com/rwanda.

Few wildlife paradises anywhere in the world are as endangered as the Virunga Volcanoes region where Volcanoes National Park is situated in a transboundary protected zone encompassing protected areas that adjoin the park in the Democratic Republic of Congo and Uganda. In the final chapter the author discusses what needs to happen to help ensure the future of Volcanoes National Park and the region as a whole.

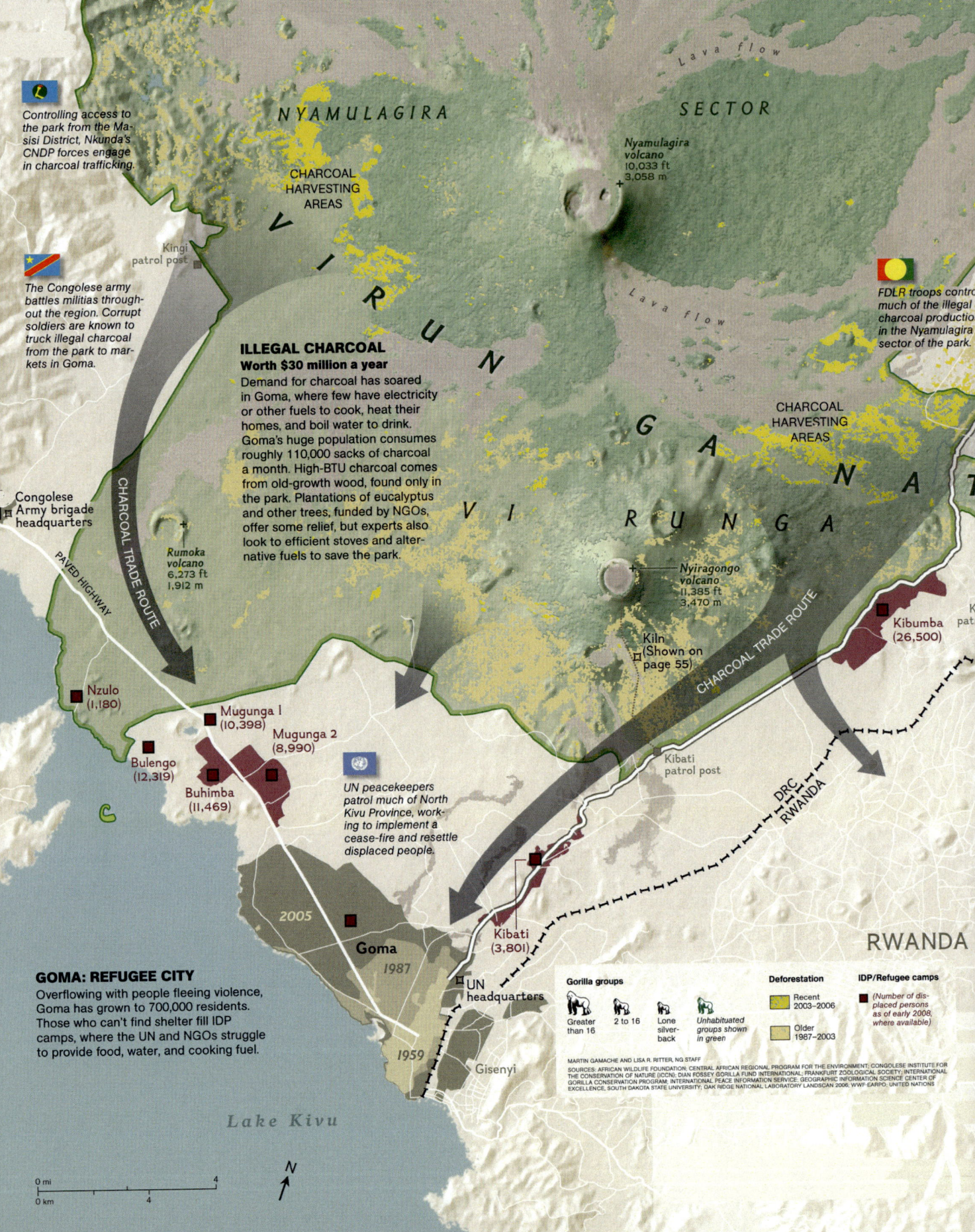

Guhonda, 43 year old silverback in the Sabyinyo Group.

Rwanda's Volcanoes National Park is a long way from home for most people who travel there. No matter how far and how long your journey, when you finally arrive and find yourself surrounded by of a magnificent family of mountain gorillas, you soon realize that all the effort was worth every minute.

Gorilla tourism in Rwanda first began late in the 1970's, thanks to all the publicity the region received from the work of gorilla researcher Dian Fossey and National Geographic magazine. Over 200,000 people from around the world have now visited the park and more are on their way. Don't let the expense and effort that is required in getting there keep you from adding the location to your travel plans. A trip to Volcanoes National Park is one of the most amazing wildlife adventures to be found anywhere in the world.

Land of the Mountain Gorilla

Deep in the heart of Africa there is a place where a conservation movement was born. The story has been told in the lives of a handful of adventurers: Captain Robert von Beringe, Carl Akeley, King Albert, George Schaller and Dian Fossey. Their adventures have been chronicled in books, a major motion picture, nature documentaries, television specials, magazine articles, newspapers and newsletters. The story is one that boggles the mind. It is one of joy, sadness, determination and sacrifice. It is a story that must never end.

A horrific genocide could have easily written the last chapter. But thanks to a small group of Rwandans and international conservationists, some of whom gave their lives, the story miraculously lives on. Fortunately for the world and for the people of Rwanda, one of Africa's conservation crown jewels is still in place.

Upon spending time in Rwanda one soon realizes how important this country is in the world today. You too will understand as you experience Volcanoes National Park and the excitement of an adventure to the land of a thousand hills. Rwandans want you to know that this is a new Rwanda. The country has a determined hope for a brighter future. Travelers to the region should consider their journeys personal investments towards helping to make that future a reality.

The Virungas

The Virungas with both extinct and active volcanoes are one of the highest mountain ranges in Africa. The elevation makes for lush valleys and mountain slopes and one of the coolest places along the equator. Recent human events make it a hotspot for conservation and political change.

As zoologists focus on the Virungas as an area of high biodiversity in need of priority funding and increased support for conservation, the United Nations and supportive countries are helping Rwanda rebuild from the destruction of the 1994 genocide.

Thanks to notable visits from former Presidents George W. Bush, Bill Clinton, First Lady Laura Bush and the voices of people like Britain's former Prime Minister Tony Blair and rock star Bono, the world is once again looking at Africa with renewed interest.

Mount Muhabura and Intore dancers.

Many scientists refer to the region as the Greater Virunga Landscape. It is composed of eight national parks, two forest reserves and two wildlife reserves. This guidebook focuses on the Rwandan part of the international mosaic. On the southeastern Rwandan side of the mountain range the park is called Volcanoes National Park (Parc National des Volcans). On the northwestern side in the Democratic Republic of Congo, the park is called Virunga National Park (Parc National des Virunga) and to the northeast in Uganda, Mahinga Gorilla National Park.

The biodiversity of the Virungas is extremely rich. Over 3,180 species of plants, 871 species of birds, 278 species of mammals, 134 species of reptiles and 84 species of amphibians have been identified. Many of these are well known, especially mega-vertebrates like the African lion, leopard, elephant, hippo, buffalo and chimpanzee. Others like the musk shrew and Congo bay owl are known to just a few.

Of particular fame and the main reason why so many people visit the area, Volcanoes National Park is home to one of the important conservation ambassadors in the world, the mountain gorilla. In fact, the inspiration of seeing these formidable creatures influenced the creation of the region as Africa's first national park. Chances are good that if you are going to Rwanda you are going to see the gorillas.

Human ambassadors also help to make Volcanoes National Park what it is today. They include park guides and trackers, researchers, volunteers, restaurant and hotel staff and the thousands of Rwandan children who make smiling and waving along roadways a national pastime.

Anyone visiting the country can easily see that every day the gorillas survive is a notable achievement in a country overwhelmed with poverty. In 2011 over 11 million people lived in Rwanda where the gross domestic product (GDP) was $583. Over 45% of the people live below the povertyline and the literacy rate is only 71%. Life expectancy is 58 years and 43% of the population is under 15 years. Given this context of economic hardship, survival of critically endangered mountain gorillas in such an impoverished part of the world offers hope for wildlife and environmental protection not just in Rwanda, but everywhere.

After Rwanda endured the terrible genocide of 1994, high in the mountains and hidden from view, over three hundred mountain gorillas were amazingly able to survive. As the rest of the world turned away, a small band of Rwandans gave their lives in protecting them. Until now the names of these men have been known to just a few, but someday when students study the history of conservation in Africa, they will be remembered as conservation heroes.

Few natural areas can exist in the 21st Century without the will and determination of dedicated people. In Rwanda the will to protect the park and the country's natural resources are a reflection of the country's heart and soul.

The Discovery

Robert Von Beringe was a German captain in 1902 when he became the first European to observe mountain gorillas on the slopes of Sabyinyo Volcano. An Austrian film company documented his life in "The Gorillas of My Grandfather". The film features Beringe's grandson Andreas Von Beringe, who a hundred years after the discovery retraces his grandfather's journey into the Virungas. The photography is superb and includes amazing aerial views and scenes of research staff visiting the park's rarely seen research groups.

Von Beringe served in Hussar Regiment No. 1 from 1894 to 1906. During the week of October 16-18, 1902, on a trip to check on German military posts in what is now the country of Burundi, Von Beringe was able to explore the Virungas. High on a ridge near Mt. Sabyinyo, at an elevation of 9,300 feet (2,834 m), he described his October 17 historic encounter with the mountain gorillas: "From our camp we saw a herd of large black apes who were trying to climb the highest point of the volcano. We succeeded in killing two large individuals. With a great rumbling noise of falling rocks, they fell into a crater opening towards the northeast. After five hours of strenuous work we managed to get one animal up on a rope. It was a large man-like ape, a male, about 5 feet (1 ½ m) high and weighing over 200 pounds (91 kg), the chest without hair, the hands and feet of huge size. I could unfortunately not determine the genus of the ape. He was of a previously unknown size for a chimpanzee and the presence of gorillas in the Lake region has as yet not been determined."

Realizing that the animals he killed were unlike anything he had ever seen and too big to be chimpanzees, he sent skeletal materials and skins to the Zoological Museum in Berlin. Today they are stored away in museum specimen containers. These specimens can be seen in the IMAX film *Mountain Gorilla*, available on DVD. At the museum Professor Paul Matschie classified the animal as *Gorilla beringei*, in honor of the man who discovered it. Today zoologists recognize two species and five subspecies of gorilla. The mountain gorilla is classified by primatologists as *Gorilla beringei beringei* (See chapter six).

A Change of Heart and the Birth of a Park

Thirty years prior to Von Beringe's discovery, the world's first national park was created in 1872 when Yellowstone National Park was established following a series of expeditions into the region. It was during this time that one of America's greatest ideas was born, the creation of the world's first national park. Members of the Washburn Expedition of 1870 were so impressed by the natural wonders they had seen that they began to propose the creation of a park to protect the area's natural wonders for all time. It was a pristine wilderness of high mountain lakes, deep river canyons, hot springs, geysers, fumaroles and mud pots inhabited by bison, elk, moose, grizzly bears, black bears and wolverines. The creation of the park was no doubt one of the most significant chapters in the history of conservation. One hundred and thirty years later, there are more than 100,000 parks, reserves and sanctuaries covering more than 12% of the Earth's surface.

Two historical figures who were inspired by Yellowstone had much to do with the establishment of Volcanoes National Park, Africa's first. Coming from different worlds, they shared an enthusiasm and love for nature. Carl Akeley was a taxidermist working for the American Museum of Natural History in New York City. Albert Leopold Clemens Marie Meinrad was the King of Belgian.

In 1921 while on a museum expedition to document mountain gorillas in the Belgian Congo, Akeley experienced a sense of great urgency on the fate of the gorillas after killing a silverback he called "The Old Man of Mikeno." As he looked into the gorilla's face he experienced an overwhelming change of heart about what he was doing and didn't want to kill any more. The expedition went on to collect four more gorillas for the museum that day, but at the same time Akeley decided that he must do something to save these gentle creatures from what could easily have been their quick demise in the years that followed.

Soon after his trip when he was the first to document motion pictures of mountain gorillas in the wild, Akeley with the support of scientists and his wife Mary petitioned the government of Belgium to protect the mountain gorilla's habitat as a national park. A Time Magazine news brief tells the story of how Mary and Dr. J. M. Derscheid were able to get an audience with the King and Queen Elizabeth so that they could be shown life size movies of the gorillas at their Belgium palace. "Graciously His Majesty permitted Mrs. Akeley to setup a portable cinema projector; and soon life-size cinema gorillas were capering, fighting, leaping high, and giving suck to their young before the gaze of King Albert and Queen Elizabeth".

As fate would have it and fortunately for the mountain gorillas, the King of Belgian, King Albert I, was an adventurer, outdoor enthusiast and nature lover. At this critical moment in the history of conservation in Africa, the King was ideally positioned as the Belgian Congo's ruling monarch.

LAND OF THE MOUNTAIN GORILLA

From 1909 to 1934 King Albert ruled the Belgian Kingdom and was well known as a mountaineer and world traveler. In 1919 the King visited national parks in the United States including Yellowstone, Yosemite and Grand Canyon. The inspiration the King received from these great parks no doubt helped convince him to follow through with Ackley's recommendation.

Albert National Park was created in 1925, just twenty-three years after German captain Robert Von Beringe became the first European to observe the mountain gorillas on the Sabyinyo Volcano. Ackeley died from dysentery in 1926 while on an expedition to further study the gorilla's habitat for the diorama he was working on in New York.

Mountain gorilla diorama in Akeley African Hall at the New York American Museum of Natural History.

Akeley's wife Mary buried him high in the mountains they had come to love at Kabara Meadow. Today, you can see the group of gorillas collected by Akeley in the Akeley African Hall in the New York American Museum of Natural History.

On February 17, 1934 in the last year of his reign, King Albert was killed during a solitary mountaineering trip, falling to his death in Belgium's mountains of Marche-les-Dames. Because of his pioneering commitment to preserving nature, King Albert could easily be considered the father of conservation in Africa.

Independence

Up until World War I, Rwanda (Ruanda) and neighboring Burundi (Urundi), were governed as part of German East Africa. During World War I Belgium occupied the country until 1918 when the League of Nations mandated the countries to Belgium as the Territory of Ruanda-Urundi. During this critical period the Belgians created a strict classification system for all Rwandans, racially separating them with identify cards as Hutu, Tutsi and Twa. Up until this time all three tribes had lived together in harmony sharing language, culture and religion. The Tutsi were elevated over the Hutu and the Twa and resentment soon began to divide the country.

From World War II to 1959 the United Nations stepped in and governed the country as a Trust Territory. That changed in 1959 when violence erupted between the Tutsi and Hutu forcing the Tutsi King to flee the country. Two years later a republic was established that was soon controlled by the Hutu-dominated Parmehutu Party.

George Schaller

At about the same time as the onset of this political change the first landmark research project on the behavior of mountains gorillas was begun by George Schaller in the Belgian Congo. Born in Germany, Schaller moved to Missouri in the United States as a young man in the 1940s. On February 1, 1959 as a graduate student at the University of Wisconsin, Schaller accompanied Dr. C. R. Carpenter to Albert National Park to begin a two-year mountain gorilla study. Carpenter returned to the United

LAND OF THE MOUNTAIN GORILLA

States six months later and Schaller and his wife remained in the uninhabited misty mountains until September 1960. They lived in an area of the park called Kabara Meadow. The meadow was a great area to observe the gorillas and Schaller observed three study groups. Today the park is called Virunga National Park and the country is called the Democratic Republic of Congo. Unfortunately, largely as the result of poaching, the mountain gorilla no longer lives in Kabara Meadow, but certainly could if security returned to the park.

The results of Schaller's research were later published by the University of Chicago Press in a detailed scientific report, *The Mountain Gorilla: Ecology and Behavior* in 1963 and in another book for the general public, *Year of the Gorilla* in 1964. Another book,

The Rwandan flag with green symbolizing prosperity and productivity, yellow wealth and blue peace and tranquility.

Gorilla: Struggle for Survival in the Virungas, is also a classic and includes outstanding photography by Michael Nichols.

Schaller's research helped the general public better understand the gentle side of gorillas and how they were by no means the terrifying beasts portrayed by early writers and in motion pictures. "No one who looks into a gorilla's eyes - intelligent, gentle, vulnerable - can remain unchanged, for the gap between ape and human vanishes; we know that the gorilla still lives within us. Do gorillas also recognize this ancient connection?" Schaller later mused, when interviewed by *National Geographic*.

Following his research on the mountain gorilla Schaller went on to become one of the world's foremost wildlife biologists. He is the author of many other important books on wildlife including books on giant pandas, tigers, Asian rhinos and African lions. In 2014 he was Vice President of Panthera, a leader in wild cat conservation.

Dian Fossey

No one person is identified more with mountain gorillas than Dian Fossey. Well known to readers of National Geographic magazine and National Geographic TV documentaries, Fossey became famous for her landmark research on gorillas from 1967 to 1985.

Many people first learned about Fossey while reading about her research and her beloved gorilla Digit in the pages of National Geographic. Magazine articles written by Fossey were published in January 1970, October 1971 and April 1981. Forty-four years later, many of these readers, including this writer, were visiting Rwanda. The story of Fossey's life was told in the movie *Gorillas in the Mist* starring Sigourney Weaver. In 2005 National Geographic published *No One Loved Gorillas More, Dian Fossey Letters from the Mist*, a book containing rare photographs of Fossey and letters to family and friends.

Fossey was not supportive of developing gorilla tourism. She felt that putting efforts into developing tourism would take away from efforts to protect the gorillas from poachers and habitat destruction. If she were alive today, after all that has happened in the region, perhaps she would have a change of heart. Tourism revenues are directed towards conservation efforts to protect the gorillas, the park, other natural areas of the country and local socio-economic community projects.

Volcanoes National Park Guide Francis Ndagijimana pointing out one of the many species of plants encountered on a gorilla trek.

Gorilla Ecotourism

In 2013 travel and tourism ranked as the largest source of export earnings followed by minerals, coffee and tea. The gorillas at Volcanoes National Park are the main attraction. In addition to gorilla tourism revenues Rwanda relies on the international community to support the long term survival of gorillas. The conservation and education efforts of the Karisoke Research Center operated by the Dian Fossey Gorilla Fund International in Musanze are great examples of the importance of this international support.

The Rwanda Development Board (formerly called Office Rwandaise du Tourisme et des Parcs Nationaux, ORTPN) headquartered in Kigali is working hard at maintaining gorilla tourism. Every year RDB sponsors a gorilla naming ceremony called "Kwita Izina" which means 'to give a name'. The event is held each year to celebrate the births of gorillas in their natural habitat. In a press release RDB states that "every birth is a confirmation of a successful conservation and protection program that will one day achieve its principle objective of removing the mountain gorilla off the endangered species list." RDB press releases and other reports are posted on their ecotourism website at www.rwandatourism.com.

World Heritage Showcase

The United Nations World Heritage program recognizes natural, cultural and historic sites around the world to be of outstanding value to humanity. Virunga National Park in the Democratic Republic of Congo on the north western side of the Virungas and parts of the Kigezi (Rukigi) Highlands of southwestern Uganda at Bwindi Impenetrable National Park, have been designated as World Heritage sites. Both areas along with Volcanoes National Park in Rwanda contain the only known habitat for mountain gorillas.

In 2014 the World Heritage List included 981 properties: 759 cultural, 193 natural and 29 mixed properties in 160 countries. Virunga National Park was designated a World Heritage Site in 1979. Bwindi Impenetrable National Park was designated a World Heritage Site in 1994.

In 1994 at the 18th Session of the World Heritage Committee, in the wake of the war in neighboring Rwanda, Virunga National Park was inscribed on the List of World Heritage Sites in Danger. As a result of the war and genocide, tens of thousands of refugees led to massive deforestation and poaching of wildlife in the park. The serious problem of poaching continues to this day and the park's staff lacks the means to adequately patrol the 650 km long boundary.

In December 1996, the World Heritage Committee had considerable discussion on the situation in the Democratic Republic of the Congo and the human tragedy unfolding there. The Committee noted that a major effort would be required over the next decade to rehabilitate and strengthen management of Virunga and to obtain local support for its conservation. With the help of a variety of institutions including the World Bank, the national government is cooperating with the World Conservation Union (IUCN) in providing technical co-operation and training assistance, the better to face current and future threats to the site.

Mount Muhabura from Virunga Lodge overlooking Lake Ruhondo.

In September 2005 a Great Ape Survival Project meeting that was held in Kinshasa, Democratic Republic of Congo, and sponsored by the United Nations Environment Program, brought together over 200 delegates. As a direct result of that conference, seventeen of twenty-three countries that have habitats for gorillas and other Great Apes formed a partnership for the long-term protection of Great Apes around the world. Renewed optimism and the recognition of the conservation challenges ahead led to the publication of the first *World Atlas of Great Apes and their Conservation,* published to help promote the cause of the Great Apes. According to the atlas the survival of great apes is threatened by:

1. Poverty of host countries – 16 out of the 23 great range states have an annual per capita income of less than US $800.

2. Growing bushmeat crisis - The atlas raises concerns over the increasing trade in great ape bushmeat and the sale of orphans to expatriates wanting to 'rescue them'. Entire groups of adults may be killed to capture one orphan for sale. In Central Africa, a single chimpanzee or gorilla carcass can fetch the equivalent of US $20-25.

3. Fragile habitats – The atlas includes maps that show the impact of infrastructure development on wildlife and GLOBIO computer model images to simulate future changes. Independent studies support these findings, predicting that if current trends in Indonesia and Malaysia persist; the orangutan will lose 47% of its habitat in the next 5 years, whilst at least 24% of the bonobo's range in the Democratic Republic of the Congo is already under logging concessions.

4. Habitat fragmentation - The atlas presents new information on the distribution of the Cross River gorilla, one of the two subspecies of western gorilla, which has only around 295 individuals left. These few animals are distributed amongst more than ten fragmented highland areas. Fragmentation isolates great ape populations from one another, increasing their vulnerability.

5. Disease - It is also increasingly clear that disease, especially Ebola hemorrhagic fever, is playing a part in the decline of ape populations and new research is needed, along with stronger efforts to limit disease transmission.

The United Nations Educational, Scientific and Cultural Organization (UNESCO) seeks to encourage the identification, protection and preservation of cultural and natural heritage around the world considered to be of outstanding value to humanity. Volcanoes National Park in Rwanda is certainly worthy of World Heritage status. However, the park can only be designated as a World Heritage Site (WHS) after being nominated by a State Party. Sites are not inscribed by UNESCO, but by the intergovernmental World Heritage Committee based on expert advice by the International Union for the Conservation of Nature (IUCN). For natural sites, their "outstanding universal value" for geological importance, biodiversity, ecosystems, or natural beauty has to be demonstrated together with their integrity.

Rwanda joined the convention in 2011. It is unlikely that Volcanoes National Park could be accepted on the list as a separate World Heritage site. First, the WHS list already contains comparable sites (Virunga, Kahuzi-Biega and Bwindi). Furthermore, the integrity of the park would be an issue as it seems unlikely that the park could survive if isolated from Virunga.

According to the ICUN it would be possible to propose a Trans boundary extension of the existing Virunga World Heritage Site (WHS). This proposal would need to be put forward by Democratic Republic of Congo, Rwanda and Uganda. One idea that is being proposed is the idea of extending Virunga National Park World Heritage Site to include Volcanoes National Park and Magahinga Gorilla Sanctuary. With Bwindi already a WHS, this could place the entire mountain gorilla range on the World Heritage list. In 2005 Uganda was spearheading this initiative by requesting international assistance from World Heritage Foundation to facilitate the process.

Let Your Journey Begin

There is no place on Earth quite like the Virungas and Volcanoes National Park. This fragile habitat is one of Africa's most amazing conservation success stories. As you prepare for your journey and a trek to see the gorillas, be mindful of the park's role as a beacon for conservation in a very troubled part of the world. Your plans to travel there will help to keep the spirit of the country's national commitment to conservation strong. Thanks for joining others who care about Rwanda, its people, its natural history and the mountain gorillas.

Rwanda is often described as the "land of a thousand hills."

20-year old Kajoriti of the Amahoro Group is missing his left hand after being injured by a poacher's snare.

Growing up in Western New York south of Buffalo and Niagara Falls, I first learned about Africa by watching the popular television program, Mutual of Omaha's Wild Kingdom. I was an avid fan of Tarzan and King Kong movies and anything else I could watch on tv or at the movies. Fortunately, today's media are much more sophisticated and accurate in their portrayals of Africa and gorillas, although movies like Peter King's 2005 King Kong remake prompt one to wonder if Hollywood will ever let go of its tall tale about the gorilla.

Over time I would go to libraries where I would read everything I could put my hands on. Today I am convinced that reading about animals played a very big part in the development of my conservation ethic.

During my freshman year in college I worked during the summer at the Buffalo Zoo and was able to visit a western lowland gorilla named Samson every day. I can still remember his distinct odor. Thanks to my days with Samson, years later, when I saw my first mountain gorillas in the wild, I was able to smell them as we approached.

One day in January, 1970 I picked up a copy of National Geographic magazine. Dian Fossey and two juvenile mountain gorillas were on the cover. After reading Fossey's writings in Geographic and later in her book Gorillas in the Mist, my passion for gorillas increased dramatically. I have been hooked ever since. I hope it happens to you too. Gorillas need our help big time.

Gorilla's Nest Lodge near park headquarters at Kinigi.

Planning Your Trip

Getting ready for a gorilla trek requires careful planning. Before you pack your bags spend some time going over everything you will need. In addition and above all, make sure you are in good physical shape. If you are planning to bring the family the minimum age to go on a gorilla trek is age 15. Hiking to see the gorillas oftentimes involves climbing straight up the sides of steep mountain slopes.

Your overall health upon arrival in Rwanda is very important. If you are nursing a cold or any other contagious illness, you could threaten the wild population. If that is the case you will need to work closely with your safari guide in dealing with the possibility of a change in plans. With fewer than 900 mountain gorillas in the world, park officials and conservationists are very concerned about the transmission of diseases between people and the gorillas. If there is any hint of a contagious illness, you will not be allowed to go on the trek.

I went on my first trip to see the gorillas in February, 1989. I joined an East Africa Wildlife Society Safari that started in Kenya and included a side trip to Rwanda. Over a three day period we visited Volcanoes National Park to the northwest and Akagera National Park in the east. We spent the night in a hotel in Kigali and arose early in the morning for the drive to park headquarters at Kinigi. We needed to be there by 7am for our briefing with park staff. After the briefing we drove to the trail head near the saddle between Mgahinga and Sabyinyo Volcanoes. Both volcanoes are inactive as are all the volcanoes in the park. The best known active volcano in Central Africa is Nyriagongo Volcano located just to the northwest and very close to gorilla habitat in the Democratic Republic of Congo's Virunga National Park.

Many people spend the night in Kigali and arise hours before sunrise to make the 7am deadline. If you are short on time you can do the same, but I recommend that you stay in Kigali on your first or last night in the country and the rest of the time stay at other accommodations close to the park. I have stayed at two hotels in Kigali and enjoyed both: the Novotel Hotel and the Hotel Milles Collins featured in the movie Hotel Rwanda.

If you have the time, spend the night near the park. Better yet, you may want to spend more than one night. You can arrange for multiple gorilla treks and spend time seeing some of the other sites in the area such as the golden monkeys or the original Karisoke research site established by Dian Fossey in 1967. There are several lodges near the park and a number of motels in Musanze. Volcanoes Safaris has some of the best accommodations both for scenic vistas and overall quality. If you want to experience a little piece of Rwandan culture while mixing with the locals consider the Hotel Muhabura in Musanze. The Hotel is a lunch and dinner hang-out for gorilla researchers and park staff and a stopover point for travelers along the road to and from Kigali.

The author spent most of his time researching this book in Rwanda while staying at the Hotel Muhabura.

    Civic groups like the Lions Club meet there too. The Musanze social scene at the hotel can include a variety of social events and dozens of people gathered around the TV enjoying a soccer match. I am sure that travel agents and Africa travel guide books have other recommendations, but in this book I want to recommend only those facilities with which I have experience with. A list of accommodations listed by the Government of Rwanda can be found in their website at www.rwandatourism.com.

    Travel between Kigali and Musanze can be an adventure in itself. The road is paved, but is extremely narrow and has little or no shoulders. Few people in Rwanda own vehicles so you will see more people walking or on bicycles than traffic. The drive takes about 90 minutes and is very scenic. Agriculture is everywhere and you will see more potato fields than anything else including many people carrying sacks of potatoes. They are on their way to or from the market in Musanze and oftentimes use bicycles to ease the burden of their loads.

Once you get past the town of Musanze, the largest community near the park, the paved road ends and the fun begins. Roads to park headquarters are very rough so be prepared for a bumpy ride. Your mode of transportation at this point of the trip must include a high clearance four wheel drive vehicle. If you are trying to save money by taking a taxi or minibus from Kigali, don't be surprised if you have problems getting to park headquarters and the trailheads where the gorilla treks begin. Some backpackers succeed in finding rides with others. If you cannot arrange for such a favor you may have to hire four-wheel drive transportation the day before. Arranging for last minute transportation can be a problem so be sure to plan. If you have not figured everything out the night before you could have a major problem in the morning.

On my first trip in 1989 gorilla tourism in Rwanda was in full swing. One difference between then and now is the number of English speaking park guides and staff at hotels and restaurants. Kinyarwanda is the primary language with French the second. In 1989 I met very few English speaking Rwandans, but today there is a big push in the country to teach English. As a result, a significant number of hotels, tour operators and park staff can speak at least some English. Most park guides are very fluent in English. Trackers, soldiers and porters speak little.

Today you will see many young children carrying English study books. When you come to Rwanda consider bringing a French-English dictionary or two. Better yet bring French-English/English-French cassette tapes or Pimsleur audio cds (English for French speakers) to give away to people you meet. Before you give something away that you brought from home always play it safe and ask for advice from your tour guide or park guide. If you really want to be generous bring a cassette or audio cd player with plenty of batteries or a power transformer. You will quickly gain a lifetime friend who when you get home will likely send you regular emails from an Internet Café.

Restrooms

Be sure to eat a light breakfast and use the restroom facility at your hotel before you head to the Kinigi park headquarters. Make sure that you know what time the hotel breakfast service begins. If you have to leave your hotel before that time, you will need to make arrangements the day before for whatever you want to eat that morning.

There are primitive restroom facilities at park headquarters in Kinigi. Take note: when you get to the trailhead you will need to ask your guide about finding the nearest tree or bushes. When nature calls on the trail to see the gorillas you cannot count on a good place to go. Definitely pack some toilet paper. If you have no choice in the matter your guide will have to assist you in finding a place that will lessen the chance of disease transmission from people to gorillas. A hole in the ground will have to be made and you will slow down your entire group. You will also no doubt end up at the back of the line. So if you have concerns about having to deal with "when nature calls" be sure to plan, plan, plan. Your trek to the gorillas may last from one hour to four hours so a light belly in the morning can only help.

Trek Food and Lunch

You will definitely want to pack some food and water for your trek. I suggest a daypack with a water bottle and a high energy snack bar or trail mix. You can ask your hotel for fresh fruit and bottled water if you failed to bring anything and there are some western style grocery stores in Kigali. Don't count on finding grocery stores stocked with every day needs like you have back home, and along the paved road to Musanze there are few opportunities to buy snacks.

When hiking, food can only be eaten when you are considered a safe distance from the gorillas. Most people hold off on eating their snacks until after they finish watching the gorillas.

You will not be able to bring your food and water during your hour with the gorillas. As you approach the group your guide will ask you to leave the food portion of your pack with the trackers. Guides and trackers have their own food and there is no need to share your food with them.

When you complete your trek you will probably be thinking of lunch. Your tour leader can take you back to your hotel or to a local restaurant like the one at the Hotel Muhabura. If you are heading back to Kigali you can also wait for lunch until you arrive if you don't mind waiting an extra two hours or more.

Medicine Chest

Be sure to pack aspirin, something for an upset stomach, diarrhea and anything else you might need along the way. Highly recommended medications to bring include anti-malarial medication, Pepto Bismol, antihistamine (diphenhydramine), Ibuprophen, Cortisone cream (helps with thistles) and antibiotic cream. Everything else can be bought within country (including antibiotics).

Watch what you eat and drink. Always drink bottled water. Soft drinks and bottled beer at the restaurant are also safe to drink.

Orientation at Park Headquarters

Upon arriving at park headquarters your tour operator will help you check in at the registration desk. Soon you will be assigned to a gorilla group and a park guide. Your group will gather around a large sign with the name of the gorilla group you will be visiting. Chances are good that you will be joined by other travelers from around the world. Group size is limited to eight people. If you prefer seeing a particular gorilla group, speak up at the registration desk and let your wishes be known. It is possible that you will be able to visit the group of your choice. RDB currently has a team of 80 trackers and anti-poachers, many of whom speak French or English. Guides will look over everyone who has shown up for the treks and try not to assign people who look out of shape to a gorilla group that requires extensive hiking. Remember, you need to be in good shape before you go on your trip to Rwanda. Mountain gorilla treks are not for people who have health problems. You must be able to climb up a steep mountain where the starting elevation may be 7,000 feet (2,133 m) or more!

All staff at the Kinigi park headquarters work for the Rwanda Development Board. Transportation from headquarters to the trailhead is provided by private transport only. Your guide will ride in whichever vehicle he arranges to ride in after he figures out which vehicles are going where.

Once your group has gathered, your park guide will brief you on what to expect on the ride to the trailhead and on the location status of your assigned gorilla group. Trackers will have already gone ahead to look for the group prior to your arrival and will communicate with your guide by radio as to how long you might expect to have to hike. On some days,

Volcanoes National Park Guide Olivier Nzabonimana telling park visitors about the Susa Group before departing park headquarters at Kinigi.

especially in May and June and September to December, when gorillas are looking for new bamboo shoots in the lower elevations, you may need to hike a very short distance before you find the gorillas. On other days you may have to hike straight up the mountain for one to four hours. If for some reason the gorillas are moving faster than normal, your group may not be able to find the gorillas at all, but this rarely happens.

During the orientation your guide will show you a picture of the group you will see showing the silverback, adult and sub adult males, females, juveniles and babies. Most will have names unless they were born after the June naming ceremony of the previous year. Copies of this group picture are usually available for sale from the registration desk. If you want a copy, ask your guide before leaving headquarters since you will probably not be able to return to this location after your trek.

Orientation at the Trail Head

Your drive to the trailhead for the beginning of your trek may take from 30 minutes to an hour. Prepare yourself for more very bumpy roads. Along the way you will see typical homes and small villages with hundreds of people. If school is not in session you will also see children of all ages, many very close to the edge of the road. Kindly do not give children gifts or candy while driving by.

When you finally arrive your guide will take you to the edge of the park where he will stop and give you the second part of your orientation. Before orientation and upon getting out of your vehicle you will be met by men who hope to be hired as porters and by children who hope you will buy something. On your trek you will be joined by a small group of trackers and soldiers. The trackers will help your group find the gorillas. The soldiers will provide extra security in case your group meets any unfriendly people along the way.

RDB does not recommend that you give away items to people at the trailhead. Upon returning from your trek you may purchase any souvenir items such as hand drawn gorilla pictures made by the children. Keep in mind that if there are many children in a group wanting to sell you something and only one child makes a sale, the other children may take away his or her money after everyone leaves. This is the main reason why RDB discourages any transactions at the trailhead.

Your guide can tell you the expected fee to hire a porter who will carry your pack and camera gear to help lighten your load. Tips are rarely discussed by park staff so if you need advice ask your tour leader. Remember to tip your trackers too. Your porter or the guide will also help you along the trail with a walking stick.

The Trek Begins

You are about to enter the park. WOW! I hope you are excited. No doubt you will have to climb over a five foot high rock wall built in 2004 and 2005 to help keep wild animals in and domestic animals out of the park. When wild animals like buffalo damage crops, many people respond by trying to go into the park illegally and kill animals. There is also a problem with people going into the park in search of water.

Planning Your Trip

As you embark on your trek try to be as quiet as possible so as not to frighten the gorillas and other wildlife. The pace of your trek will be determined by the amount of vegetation the trackers have to cut to make a path and the overall physical condition of your group. If anyone is not able to keep up with the pace, the guide will slow everyone down. Once the group figures out who is the slowest encourage that person to move to the front of the line closest to the guide. The last thing you want is to pressure the slowest member of the group to overextend him or herself and then stumble and fall down and get hurt. Remember, if that happens everyone in the group will be affected.

Your guide will point out a very important plant species that everyone on the trek needs to know about, stinging nettles. You will want to avoid contact with this plant at all times since the sharp nettle leaves can inflict a painful sting. If you get stung the pain will eventually subside, but only after several hours of itching and discomfort. That's why wearing rubber hiking boots and thick pants and gloves is so highly recommended on all treks.

Sabyinyo Group members showing concern about the approach of the lone silverback Nyakalima.

Approaching the Gorillas

As you approach the gorilla group your guide will begin making low grunting sounds to help assure the gorillas that friendly people are approaching. You may also hear gorilla vocalizations and the sounds of breaking vegetation as the group moves through the forest. At this point your guide will ask everyone to leave their daypacks with the trackers and porters. You will be able to take only your camera gear. Make sure that the flash mechanism on your camera has been turned off. Flash photography is strictly prohibited since it agitates the gorillas. You will have a maximum of one hour to view the gorillas. During this time you may take as many pictures as you like including video.

As you move closer to the group individual gorillas may need to pass very close to where you are standing. Juveniles and babies may even try to approach you. Any time the gorillas get too close your guide will ask you to step back to keep a safe distance. Sometimes the gorillas will want to walk past you within just a few feet and you may not be able to move back. If this happens remain calm and follow the directions of your guide. Do not show any fear and do not point at the gorillas or look directly into the gorillas' eyes. Any of these actions can frighten them. Visitors are asked to maintain a distance of 22 feet (7 m) from the gorillas.

Other important park rules that you are asked to follow include:

- Spitting in the park is strictly prohibited.
- If you need to cough, cover your mouth and turn away from the gorillas.
- When with the gorillas, keep your voice low.
- Try not to make rapid movements that may frighten the gorillas.
- If a gorilla should charge or vocalize at you, do not be alarmed, stand still, look away from the gorilla and follow your guide's directions.
- Do not litter.

Most trekkers visit the gorillas only once, making the trip a lifetime experience. Let me offer a word of advice. Since you may never return and experience these moments again, try not to take pictures at every turn. Snap a few images and then put the camera away. You can purchase some great books when you return and there are a number of superb photographs and videos on the market. Absorb the moment. Everyone comes away from the experience inspired in a special way. Relax, immerse yourself in the forest and use all your senses in exploring your surroundings. Look up, down and all around. Listen, smell, touch carefully and enjoy. Cameras will bring back many memories, but the best memories are stored not on disk or film, but in your mind, heart and soul.

Gorilla Trek Checklist

You will want to come prepared with at least the following items:

- ☐ Gorilla trek permit from RDB (see note below).
- ☐ Your passport and money is probably best brought with you than left in the safari vehicle or in your hotel.
- ☐ Bring plenty of Rwanda money to tip guides and trackers (ask your trip leader for suggested amounts).
- ☐ Sturdy and waterproof hiking shoes.
- ☐ Nice clothing: Rwandans take pride in their dress and you should too, dress smart.
- ☐ Protective thorn-proof covers and gloves for your hands, legs and arms that are thorn proof. Dress in layers.
- ☐ Lightweight rain jacket.
- ☐ Day pack, water and snacks.
- ☐ Small first aid kit.
- ☐ Journal for note taking and recording your thoughts.
- ☐ Lightweight walking stick (your guide can make you one on the spot).
- ☐ Toilet paper.
- ☐ Plastic water bottles: Do not give bottles to children. Some will use them to sniff fumes from liquids like gasoline.

Photography Tips

- ☐ Camera with shut-off control for flash (tripods are not allowed, they can scare the gorillas).
- ☐ Bring more film or disk space on your digital camera Flash Disk than you think you will need. Bring at least one extra Flash Disk just in case and an extra battery.
- ☐ Always ask for permission before taking pictures of people.
- ☐ Don't go overboard with your camera, enjoy the moment.

Weather Conditions

Always be prepared for rain. Rwandans say they have two seasons, the rainy season and the not so rainy season.

Rwanda Phone and Internet Directory

Rwanda Development Board Tourism Website
www.rwandatourism.com

Gorilla Permits

Most people have their tour leader arrange for permits in advance. If you are traveling on your own, you can also book your permit through the Rwanda Development Board offices (RDB) in Kigali or Musanze.

Fees for Mountain Gorilla Permits:

The fee for gorilla visits as of June 1, 2014 was $750 per person for non-nationals, $375 for foreign residents and 30,000 FRW for Rwandan citizens.

Rwanda Development Board (RDB)
Boulevard de l'Umuganda, Gishushu, Nyarutarama Road
PO Box 6239
Kigali, Rwanda
Tel (250) 252 580388
Email: info@rdb.rw
http://www.rdb.rw

Geology of Volcanoes National Park

Large black volcanic boulders form part of the park's south eastern boundary in the shape of an impressive rock wall. The 39 mile (63 km) perimeter fence is about 6 feet (1.83 m) high and 4 feet (1.22 m) wide and helps to deter both forest buffalo and mountain gorillas from straying into the gardens of local communities. Much of the rock is what geologists call extrusive igneous, lava that cooled quickly above ground. As I climb over the wall I am careful to watch my footing. The last thing I want to happen is to fall and hurt myself. I have come too far to see this part of paradise.

Most of the rock forming Volcanoes National Park is very old. With the exception of a minor eruption on Mount Bisoke in 1957, the volcanoes are largely inactive. The situation outside the park to the southwest, in the Democratic Republic of the Congo (DRC), is much different. In the DRC at Virunga National Park there are some very active volcanoes. Most recently Nyamuragira Volcano erupted during the month of March, 2012.

A rock wall perimeter fence helps to define the park boundary.

Looking north from the Virunga Lodge at Lake Bulera.

Geology of Volcanoes National Park

The Virunga volcanoes lie about 100 miles south of the Equator in the northwest corner of Rwanda. This is the Great Lakes Region of Central Africa. Lake Victoria, the largest lake in Africa and the second largest in the world, is 150 miles (241 km) to the east. Lake Tanganyika, the world's longest lake, is 130 miles (209 km) to the south. Closer by are smaller lakes fed by the park's mountain runoff. Lake Tshahafi and Lake Mugisha are just across the border in Uganda. Lake Bulera and Lake Ruhondo are just east of Musanze. To the southwest, Lake Kivu is the highest lake in Africa at 4,829 ft (1,472 m) forming the southeast border of Rwanda with the DRC.

Other mountains in the region include the Mitumba Massif forming the west side of the Rift Valley and to the north, the spectacular Ruwenzori Mountains forming part of the border between Uganda and the DRC. The Ruwenzori's are the famous "Mountains of the Moon," long thought to be the source of the Nile. Today we know of two sources of the Nile, the Ruwenzori's and the Kagera River basin which lies mainly in Rwanda and includes Akagera National Park.

The Great Rift Valley is a vast area created over time by the gradual separation of the African and Arabian tectonic plates. Geologists use the term *rift* to describe places where the earth has been literally torn apart. The East African rift system is geologically complex, with two separate rift branches along the equator. The Virungas are part of the western rift, locally called the Albertine Rift named for King Albert. Forming the western side of the Rift Valley, the Albertine Rift is located in five countries and stretches north to south from Lake Albert in Uganda, south into Rwanda, the DRC, Burundi and Lake Tanganyika in Tanzania.

The rift is the low-elevation area around Lake Edward. The mountains on the rift shoulder form a series of mountain chains separating the forest-savannas of East Africa in Kenya and Tanzania from the Guineo-Congolian rainforest of Central Africa. The rift owes its existence to the uplifting of the earth's crust and volcanic activity during the formation of the Great Rift Valley and the famous valley lakes. According to geologists this all took place during the mid-Pleistocene Epoch about 1,600,000 years ago and ending roughly 10,000 years ago.

Eight major volcanoes form the Virunga Conservation Area and extend twenty-five miles from the DRC north through Rwanda and Uganda. Three of them, Mount Nyriagongo at 11.385 ft (3,470 m), Mount Nyamuragira at 10,033 ft (3,058 m) and Mount Mikeno at 14,557 (4,437 m), are located solely in Virungas National Park in the DRC. Mount Karisimbi at 14,787 ft (4,507 m), the highest peak in the range, and Mount Bisoke (also called Visoke) at 12,175 ft (3,711 m) are located on the border of DRC and Rwanda. Diane Fossey established her research camp in a saddle area between Visoke and Karisimbi and named it Karisoke.

Lake of lava in the Nyiragongo Crater.

Another peak, Mount Sabyinyo at 11,923 ft (3, 634 m), the oldest of the eight peaks, is located partially in DRC, Rwanda and Uganda. The two northernmost peaks, Mgahinga at 11,398 feet (3,474 m) and Muhavura at 13,540 ft (4,127 m), are located along the border of Volcanoes National Park and Mahinga Gorilla National Park in Uganda. With the exception of Mount Nyriagongo (major eruptions in 2002) and Mount Nyamuragira (major eruptions in 2012), most of the eight volcanoes are dormant.

The region is also made up of Precambrian rock interspersed with the volcanic deposits. Geologists say that the volcanoes were created about two million years ago when they erupted periodically during the Pliocene and Pleistocene. As the volcanoes spread lava, volcanic ash and pumice across broad areas, the rocks that formed were created in layers.

North and South America have a shared geological history with Africa. Look at a globe and see the excellent fit between the Gulf of Guinea on the west coast of Africa and the east coast of Brazil in South America. The more one studies the geology of the continents, the clearer one can see the relationship between them. Similar pieces of the puzzle can be seen when looking at the shape of continents between eastern North America and northwest Africa, North Africa and Europe, Madagascar and India and southeast Africa and Antarctica. Geologic evidence combined with the study of anthropology and paleontology provides strong evidence for the existence of a one time *super continent* called Pangaea.

The word Pangaea comes from the Greek meaning "all earth". The enlightened traveler to Rwanda can look at a trip to Africa almost like part of a study of prehistoric times. We certainly have a stronger relationship with this part of the world than most people think.

During the Pleistocene, when the volcanoes in the park were still active, woolly mammoths, rhinos, giant sloths and saber-toothed tigers roamed the North America continent. Eventually they all went extinct with the last mammoths surviving up to 8,000 years ago. During this same geologic period Africa's megafauna were able to survive. Many believe that humans crossing the Bering Strait from Asia caught North America's Pleistocene fauna off guard by the sudden appearance of humans. African animals on the other hand had already adapted to humans. This theory supports archaeological evidence indicating that humans first inhabited Africa and why Pleistocene fauna still survives in Africa today.

This is the land of a thousand hills. The hills and valleys are largely intact, but the same cannot be said for the area's biodiversity. To make room for agriculture native people have destroyed most of the ancient forests and the wildlife. What trees remain outside protected areas are largely exotic species like eucalyptus and cypress trees. Where gorillas and other creatures once roamed there are now millions of people raising beans and potatoes.

Dry Lava Zones

In the area where over two million people live alongside the boundary of the Virunga Conservation Area, the volcanic soils are very porous. Here rainwater quickly soaks into the ground leaving little water available near the surface. The water eventually emerges at lower elevations, but this is of little help to the people living in the dry lava zone in areas like park headquarters at Kinigi. Because of the geology people have to walk long distances for water. Sometimes they cross into the park to collect water from springs, streams, swamps and lakes in the forest. When they do, trees are cut down for fuel and animals are hunted for bushmeat. This kind of activity affects the gorillas and other forest creatures when they are injured or killed by guns, arrows, or snares.

The United States Forest Service (USFW) and the African Wildlife Foundation (AWF) have been providing technical assistance to the region in hopes that water systems can be developed to help people living near the park improve their quality of life while decreasing human impacts. This can be achieved by drilling more wells and by building water catchment devices to collect rainwater. A recent survey conducted by USFW and AWF found that there is an overall lack of leadership for providing water resource management for the communities near the park. A number of government agencies are collecting information relating to the watersheds in the area, but the information is not centralized and the key players are not communicating with each other.

Anyone wanting to help protect the park can explore opportunities to help people improve their ability to obtain water. In 2006, a glimmer of hope was profiled on the Internet at Yahoo.com with the story of Richard Bangs. Humanitarians like Bangs hope that by providing reliable sources of fresh water for people living in nearby communities, people will be discouraged from illegal activities in the park.

Because so many people go into the park to search for water, DFGFI is working with RDB and the communities to construct rain barrel catchments. They have put in five 10,000L tanks at the Bisate Clinic, two 10,000L tanks at Bisate School and tanks at the trackers house. They have also set up a community catchment system for Bisate with a massive cistern which will service thousands of people.

Protecting water resources in and around the Virungas is important to both people and wildlife. Overland water flow and erosion have increased because of deforestation. The rate of water filtering into the ground is higher where the forest floor is intact and well developed. Through this natural phenomenon the forest functions as an important filter helping to soak the water into the soil. When the forest is eliminated more water flows out of the area making less water available for people and wildlife.

If communities in the region are to have stable and economical water supplies, protection of the remaining forests in the Virungas is critical. Therein is one of the greatest conservation challenges facing the park. People need to understand why the forest must be protected and water that is available close to the surface from wells and catchment devices must be made accessible.

Uncontrolled erosion resulting from deforestation has many other consequences besides depleting the available underground water supply. There are also soil stability problems that can severely decrease the biological productivity of the soil. Organizations like the DFGFI and AWF have educational programs underway to help people understand these realities, but they need more support.

Mount Karisimbi

From a satellite photo it is easy to see how expansive the top of Mount Karisimbi is compared to the other Virunga volcanoes. At the top there is a ¾ mile (1.2 km) wide crater called Muntango. As the highest peak Karisimbi is occasionally covered with a white layer of hail and sleet. In the native language of Kinyaruanda the name comes from *nsimbi* meaning white shell.

George Schaller and Dian Fossey both spent time studying mountain gorillas in a meadow called Kabara located in the saddle area between Mount Karisimbi and Mt. Mikeno in the DRC. Fossey described the upper part of the cone as surrounded with large Alpine meadow rings that were barren and moonlike. Today the summit attracts dedicated mountain climbers from around the world. There is no main trail up the steep mountain and good navigation skills are required. The trip takes two days and requires a park guide and a permit from RDB.

If you are going to Rwanda to hike to the top of some of the volcanoes, remember that in Rwanda there are two seasons: the rainy season and the not so rainy season. Others say that there are two dry seasons from June to September and December to February. Just remember that the world's climate is changing and you can't always count on historical trends.

Geologists describe Karisimbi as a complex volcano called a stratovolcano, one that is tall and steep, conical in shape and made up of both hardened lava and volcanic ash. Compared to the rest of the volcanoes in the Virungas, Karisimbi is considered relatively young with the last estimated eruption to have occurred in 8050 BC.

Much of what is known about the life and ecology of the mountain gorilla comes from studies of gorilla groups living on the slopes of Karisimbi. The northern slopes of Karisimbi and the adjacent southern slopes of Bisoke provide habitat for one of the highest densities of gorillas in the world. Many travelers coming to see the gorillas trek to the southwest slope of Karisimbi to see the Susa Group, once the largest of the groups habituated for tourism.

Mount Bisoke

On many maps, books and other publications you may see Mount Bisoke written as Mount Visoke. Visoke is a Swahili pronunciation of Bisoke. The letter B in the Kinyarwanda language becomes V in Swahili. Bisoke was originally known as Bushokoro.

Crater Lake on the top of Mount Karisimbi.

No matter what you call the mountain if you are in shape and up for a daylong climb, on a clear day the view from the top is incredible. There is a 1,476 foot (450 m) wide crater lake at the summit. If you are able to approach the north flank, you might be able to see two small cones that were created after a minor eruption in 1957.

The mountain top is covered with giant senecio plants, an endemic species that can reach twelve feet tall and grow for several hundred years. Local people sometimes cut down these ancient relics for firewood. Both government approved guides and permits are required from RDB for authorization to climb Mount Bisoke.

Volcanoes National Park is divided into a variety of management zones with no fixed boundaries. The research zone is between Mount Karisimbi and Bisoke. The tourism zone is at Bisoke and between Bisoke and Sabyinyo. You can hike into the research zone to the original Karisoke Research Camp with a park guide, but tourists are not allowed to visit the research gorilla groups.

Mount Sabyinyo

Sabyinyo is well known to travelers who have come to see the gorillas that live on its slopes. Group 11, now thought to be disbanded or in the DRC or Uganda, used to live on the Rwanda side of the mountain and was seen by many gorilla trekkers during the 1980s. There are several habituated groups in this area, the most popular being the Sabyinyo group.

The name Sabyinyo means "old man's teeth" for the jagged ridges on the summit. The mountain also holds the distinction of being in all three countries in this tri-national protected area including parts of Rwanda, DRC and Uganda.

Mount Mgahinga

The town of Musanze is less than 10 miles south of Mount Mgahinga and the tri-national border with the DRC and Uganda. The northern side of Mgahinga is home to the mountain gorillas of Uganda's Mgahinga National Park. The park encompasses 13 square miles (33.7 km^2) and contains a small population of mountain gorillas including one group that has been habituated for tourism called Nyakagezi.

Mount Mgahinga.

In Uganda the mountain is called Mount Gahinga. Local people call small piles of stones in their gardens "gahinga". It is easy to see how the name came about when comparing the peak to the taller Mount Muhavura to the north. The volcano once had a crater lake on top, but over time, the lake has turned into a lush swamp.

Mount Muhavura

Mount Muhabura towers over the Kisoro District in Uganda. As the dominant landmark in the area the name means 'the guide." To hike this peak you need a permit from Mount Mgahinga National Park in Uganda. From the top you can see spectacular views of the Virungas, Lake Edward in Uganda's Queen Elizabeth National Park, Bwindi National Park and the Ruwenzori Mountains. There is a field of giant lobelia and

Giant lobelias growing along the crater rim on the top of Mount Mgahinga.

senecio on top. Mount Muhabura is the driest of the volcanoes and is considered by many to be a sacred mountain.

The best views of the Virungas are seen during the dry season from January-February and June-August. For some excellent aerial views make sure you get a DVD copy of the IMAX film "*Mountain Gorilla*".

One of the best ways to understand the Virunga landscape is to download the free computer program, Google Earth. Using this program you can zoom in and fly over the entire ecosystem including the surrounding areas of habitat and human settlement in the DRC, Rwanda and Uganda. Key in the word Rwanda and explore the region's volcanoes, lakes and forests. Your understanding of the park and its geology will be enhanced and you will gain a much greater appreciation for the Virunga landscape.

Satellite images help to give a clearer picture of how extensive agriculture is in all three countries that surround the park. As you "Google" the landscape you can also check out the active volcanoes in the region at Mt. Nyriagongo and Mt. Nyamuragira. Use the vertical zoom tool to tilt and view the mountain relief so you can imagine flying over the park. When you can see everything in perspective it will help you to understand how what happens outside the park is important to the protection of the ecosystem as a whole.

I met Frances in 1989 at the Kigali Airport. I was on my first safari with a group of birdwatchers on a two country tour that included trips to the Masai Mara Reserve in Kenya and Volcanoes National Park in Rwanda. Frances was our driver and guide and I remember him as being friendly and full of enthusiasm. I have a video of him driving us from the airport and on into the highlands of the Virungas. He was the first Rwandan I ever met. I often wonder what happened to Frances during the civil war and the genocide that followed. I wish that I had called the White House or made even a feeble attempt at asking my government to intervene, but like most Americans I felt helpless as I watched the horrors of 1994 unfold on TV. One traveler accurately described the world's reaction after he visited the Ntarama Church where over 5000 people died. It was "a bizarre reminder of the 100 days that history tried to ignore".

Roz Carr author of "Land of a Thousand Hills" and one of the most amazing ladies I have ever met, aptly describes Rwandans in the warmest possible way- "the people are so gentle". Indeed, over the years I have met Rwandans from all over the country and from many walks of life. Every person I have had the pleasure of meeting radiated a kind and gentle spirit.

Rwandans are hard working and determined. Today I am proud to say that I have friends in Rwanda.

There are countless ways visitors to Rwanda can get involved in supporting the country's youth.

The People of Rwanda

You can learn about Rwanda's people and culture in many ways. Most books and magazine articles have been written by Western writers. Recommended titles are highlighted in the bibliography. To get the latest thinking directly from Rwanda you should go online and read articles written by Rwandans themselves. My favorite place for Rwanda news on the Internet is a newspaper called The New Times located at www.newtimes.co.rw.

When touring Rwanda plan on visiting museums and memorials and look into going on a culture tour. One of the ways you can show your respect for the Rwandan people is to visit a Genocide Memorial. These sites are very difficult to write about yet alone visit. For example, on April 14, 1994 over 5,000 people were killed by death squads when they sought refuge inside the grounds and buildings of the Ntarama Church. Bullet holes still dot the ceiling, bloodstains can be seen smeared on the walls and thousands of skulls have been put on display in a massive underground display.

The Murambi Memorial Centre is the site of a school where 27,000 people were killed. Hundreds of corpses are still temporarily preserved and on display. The experience of visiting a memorial will touch you in a tremendous way and cause you to want to make some effort to help make our world a better place for future generations. To learn more about genocide memorials and some incredible survivor stories visit www.kilgalimemorialcentre.org.

Many people enjoy visiting the local markets of Rwanda like the ones in Kigali and Musanze. At these markets you will see buyers and sellers offering vegetables, goat meat, bananas and all kinds of other items. Don't be shocked by the sight of seeing a rack full of goat heads and other cuts of meat. Nothing goes to waste in this country where the average annual income is a little over $200.

Outside of Kigali there is a market devoted almost entirely to banana beer. Narad Mathura writes in VirtualTourist.com that the "large Nyabugogo Marche is open every day, but is biggest on weekends. Any and everything can be bought and unlike Rwandan villages and cities it is located in a valley! It's safe to walk around, but a bit far from the city center so a minibus or motorcycle taxi should get you there for no more than 40 cents US. Lots of people trying to sell, but no hassles like other African touristy places, take usual cautions."

Over the past few years Rwanda's hopes for the future have been bolstered by the growing number of celebrities and political leaders who have made visits to the country. Since 1998 former President Bill Clinton has visited Rwanda on an almost annual basis. In July 2005 he pledged more support for fighting AIDS and once again offered his regret for failing to stop the 1994 Genocide. He first admitted failure in his autobiography, *My Life*, when he said "the failure to try to stop Rwanda's tragedies became one of the greatest regrets of my presidency."

In 1998 when Clinton was still president, he was the first western leader to own up to the world's failure to stop the genocide. Since then, through the Clinton Foundation, he has stayed involved by supporting his global anti-Aids initiative. According to an article in Rwanda's The New Times, "...despite his indifference during the killings in which an estimated one million Tutsis and Hutu moderates perished, Clinton still commands big respect among Rwandans."

The Gisozi Memorial Education Center in Kigali is the burial site of over 250,000 people killed in a three month period during the genocide. Clinton laid a wreath when he visited that memorial and museum in 2006. In his Africa Travel Journal he wrote "Our young guide lost his big brother and sister-in-law -- six family members in all. Photos of countless children were displayed, all of whom were murdered in the genocide. No visitor to the memorial could ever forget what happened in 1994. I hope that it will ensure that it will not happen again, and I am honored to have played a small role in its construction."

When First Lady Laura Bush visited in 2005 she urged Rwandans not to lose hope and drew a parallel to the 1994 genocide with U.S. history when she said "we haven't totally moved on from slavery 130 years after the Civil War." On a trip through Africa Bush visited Rwandan President Paul Kagame and spent time promoting U.S. efforts to help the country fight AIDS and to support programs designed to help girls get an education.

Most of the people I met in researching this book worked at Volcanoes National Park. They were RDB employees at Volcanoes National Park, at RDB headquarters in Kigali, Karisoke Research Center staff with the Dian Fossey Gorilla Fund International and hotel staff in Kigali, Kinigi and Musanze. In the capital city of Kigali I met members of the Rotary Club of Kigali-Virunga and an assortment of people connected to international charities or ecotourism.

Members of the Rotary Club in Kigali recently took on a monumental task in building the country's first public library. These ambitious and industrious Rotarians hope that the "tools used for destruction will be replaced with tools of knowledge." For many years, Rotarians have been active in efforts to reduce illiteracy, from building schools and paying salaries of teachers to serving as tutors while adding such activities as collecting and distributing books and audiovisual materials to libraries. Rotarians are working with governments to create large-scale replicable literacy projects in the developing world. Thanks to Rotary, the library in Kigali now open to the public (www.rls.gov.rw).

Typical Rwandan homes along the edge of the park.

Considerable progress has been made in recent decades in reducing illiteracy, yet close to a billion people lack the most basic literacy and numeracy skills. Millions more are functionally illiterate, lacking the skills necessary to meet the demands of everyday life. UNESCO, the energetic United Nations children's advocate, illuminates some of the greatest challenges for those tackling illiteracy:

-Ninety-eight percent of the world's illiterate population is in developing countries.
-Fifty percent of the world's illiterate people live in India and China.
-More than 50 percent of the population of Africa is illiterate.
-Two-thirds of all those who lack literacy and numeracy skills are women.
-More than 130 million school-age children are not attending classes.

The People of Rwanda

One of the havens of this illiteracy is in the rural areas. The Rwandans I met at Karisoke and at the park helped me to understand the country's largely rural population. They were very friendly and did not hold back in answering my many questions. Staff and researchers working at the park and for the Karisoke Research Center live in the nearby communities of Gisenyi or Musanze, and so they are intimately familiar with the local issues and conditions.

People in the rural areas surrounding the park live very simple lives. Homes are round, dark and windowless with walls of stick and mud. Each is topped with a thatch roof shaped like a cone. An open fire burns inside with black smoke billowing skyward. Almost every home is surrounded by a variety of different crops including corn, beans and potatoes. Children congregate everywhere and are easily seen near the roadway. Many are very small children who look just a few years old.

Children watching for travelers along roadways help to make waving a national pastime.

Guide to Rwanda's Volcanoes National Park

As you drive to the park you will see thousands of people walking. Very few have cars. The most common form of transportation is the bicycle and most who can afford one use it to transport vegetables and other goods to and from town.

For most villagers the day starts at 6:00am. A typical breakfast includes sorghum or banana beer for adults and sorghum porridge for children. Breakfast is typically followed by a day in the fields, including taking care of crops and livestock including cows, goats and sheep. During the rest of the day meals include potatoes, beans, meats, sweet potatoes and corn. Later, the people enjoy visiting with each other telling stories and dancing to Rwandese music. Most evenings are spent listening to the radio.

Intore dancers.

In both small and large towns, mainly near paved highways, many Rwandans live in modest rectangular homes with cement block walls and tin roofs. Homes are very simple with sparse furniture. However, some amenities are hardly taken for granted in this environment. For example, dependable electricity is a big problem in Rwanda.

Rwandans take pride in how they are dressed and I was impressed to see so many people wearing clothes that looked like they were well taken care of. Whenever I saw a man wearing a sports jacket and tie in a world surrounded by poverty, I was reminded that no matter where one lives, in a simple hut or a nice home, one can still choose to look good and take pride in his or her appearance.

Story Telling

Like people everywhere Rwandans enjoy telling stories and the gorilla trackers and guides I met had plenty. Park Guide Olivier Nzabonimana told me a memorable story involving Kurira the dominant silverback from the Susa Group. One day he watched as a baby in the group tried to play with Kurira. The silverback showed little interest until he finally gave up and picked up the baby in his arms in much the same way that a human father would. For the next five minutes Kurira played with the baby and Olivier was amazed at how humanlike the scene looked. Finally Kurira put the baby down and when he did all the other babies in the group tried to get the same kind of treatment. Kurira was overwhelmed until he finally gave up and walked away.

Fidele Nsengiyumva works as a tracker. He told me how one day he saw Guhonda, the dominant silverback in the Sabyinyo Group, come across a snare. Snares are illegal in the park and are used to catch antelope. On many occasions gorillas end up getting caught resulting in serious injuries. Unless the park's Mountain Gorilla Veterinary Project Team is able to intervene, injuries can lead to death. When Guhonda found the snare, Fidele saw him steer other members of his group away and then push vegetation at the trap until it triggered. What followed next really caught Fidele by surprise. Guhonda picked up the snare and threw it towards the trackers as if to say, there, here's another one you can take out of my forest!

Art and Music

Art is also important to Rwandans. Basket weaving skills indicate a family's social status. A variety of baskets are available for sale at markets and in hotel gift shops. Ask your tour guide for shopping tips in the nearby business district. Look carefully at labels or ask the person trying to sell you something where the souvenir you are considering was made. Many items for sale in hotel gift shops are made in Kenya, so if you want authentic Rwandan art, check for the country of origin.

Rwandese music includes singing and drums. Musicians and dancers are just as passionate about their performances as anywhere else. On my last trip to the country I was able to catch an enthusiastic group of drummers and dancers performing for dignitaries at the Hotel Novetel. The woman dancers were elegantly dressed in bright colored dresses and moved gracefully to the beat of the male drummers. I have also been fortunate to enjoy drummers and dancers at a Karisoke Research Center celebration. Rwandans love playing drums and I had a lot of fun joining in at one of the DFGFI celebrations I attended near the park. Don't be shy in asking to participate. Rwandans are proud of their culture.

Homemade xylophones and stringed instruments are popular and dancing ceremonies with swaying and hopping celebrate friendship, thanks, birth, marriage, death, harvest and hunting. Combining the sounds of Reggae, country and Congo sounds results in a nice African blend intermixed with historical and local folklore. However, each region in the country has its own special music and dance. Traditions include Intwatwa, Umushayayo, Imparamba and Ikinimba (folklore). In fact, UNESCO was so impressed by Rwanda's national dance as to officially declare it one of the world's Unique Cultural Heritages.

The "Anthology of World Music: Africa - Music from Rwanda" CD with Cecile Kayirebwa features music from various tribes including Tutsi, Hutu and Twa. Cecile Kayirebwa was born in Kigali, Rwanda, in 1946, and is one of the founding members of the *Rwanda Song and Dance Circle*. This association prompted her to begin composing and singing and she soon began appearing on *Radio Rwanda*.

DFGFI staff performs at a party celebrating the support of the Partners in Conservation Program that visits the park annually from the Columbus Zoo in Ohio.

"Testimony from Rwanda", another collection of authentic Rwandan music, by Samputu includes soaring ballads, village celebrations and Congolese dance music. Songs of praise and traditional dance music include "Rehema", which tells the story of a Christian man who falls in love with a Muslim girl, and "Beautiful Rwanda".

Sports

Soccer (football) is Rwanda's most popular sport. Basketball and volleyball are catching on, but more than likely if you are in a public place with a TV people will gather to watch soccer. President Paul Kagame has made the development of soccer one of his highest priorities. In 2006 the FIFA World Cup team called the Wasps knocked

President Paul Kagame speaking at the United Nations.

out Namibia 4-1 helping Rwanda gain 20 places to 104th in the world rankings - the highest the country has ever been. In 2012 Rwanda was represented in the London Olympics with seven athletes, three in track and field, one in mountain biking, one in Judo, and two in swimming. Rwanda's most successful Olympian, Mathias Ntawulikurua made the final of the 10,000 m at the 1996 Atlanta Games. He also competed in the marathon in both Sydney and Athens, finishing 15th and 62nd respectively.

Education

Rwanda is working hard to educate more of its citizens. Education is free at the primary level and according to UNICEF 78 percent of students reach the fifth grade. It is very unfortunate that most families cannot afford to either provide the school supplies and uniforms that their children need to go to school or for their education after the fifth grade. The school year runs from January to October. Over the past ten years primary school enrollment has increased from about 60% to over 82%.

Currently there are twelve institutions of higher learning in Rwanda with a student enrollment of over 10,000. The largest of these, the National University of Rwanda in Butare has an enrollment of over 8,000. The government is working on ways to enroll many more students in the years to come. Plans are underway to turn the country into Africa's technology hub in hopes that information and communication technologies will help to boost economic growth.

Communication Tips

Hand Shaking: When you meet a Rwandan, hand shaking is an acceptable way to meet. Shake hands mainly with men. In urban areas shaking hands with women is also acceptable. The older person should always initiate the gesture and you should shake hands lightly unless you are close in age to the person you are meeting. Men are often seen holding hands with other men, which is a common sign of friendship.

Languages: Rwandans mainly speak Kinyarwandan. Most people you meet at tourist destinations also speak French and some English. There is a big push to teach more English in the country as evidenced by school children carrying English language books and by their eagerness to greet you in English.

Questions about one's tribe: You should not ask people about the tribe they are from and only ask questions about the war after you have started a friendship. You can ask how was the genocide and how did you survive. A good way to carry on a conversation about the war is to tell the person you are talking to that you are sorry that it happened and wish the country well.

Gifts for Children: The best way to give gifts to children is to do it in an organized way. Ask your guide for advice. Gifts of pens, paper and books are better than giving money.

Other Gifts: French-English pocket dictionaries make great gifts and cassette players that can be donated to the schools are greatly appreciated. Contact DFGFI or RDB for help with distribution.

Kinyarwanda Expressions:
Mwaramutse (Good morning)
Bite? (Hello)
Muraho (How are you?)
Witwande? (What's your name?)
Nitwa (My name is ...)
Murakoze (Thank you)

Religion

Rwandans have freedom of religion as guaranteed by the Rwandan Constitution. Public meetings are regulated by the government and anyone who interferes with a religious ceremony is subject to being fined or imprisoned. Public schools allow religious instruction oftentimes reflecting the denomination of the founders of the school. The dominant religions are Protestant, Catholic and Muslim.

Food

Typical foods include bananas, legumes, sweet potatoes, maize, cassava and potatoes. Hotel fare includes chicken, beef, fish and pasta dishes often with French fries or rice. It is not recommended to drink water unless it is bottled. Eating uncooked food including fruits and vegetables can also be a problem.

Locally available foods include matoke (mashed green banana), spaghetti, boiled potatoes, chips and rice, vegetables and sauce. Goat meat is also available. For breakfast many restaurants serve chapatti (flatbread) and chai (tea).

Kigali has the greatest variety of restaurants including Chinese, Greek, French, Indian, Italian and Ethiopian. An Italian restaurant overlooking the city called New Cactus has an extensive pizza menu. Don't miss the Lake Victoria grilled fish and fresh tilapia stuffed with herbs from local gardens. Some of the best food including breakfast with omelets and all kinds of desserts can be found in the upscale hotels like the Hotel Des Milles Collines, Raico Hotel and Serena Hotel.

Holidays and Festivals

January 1, New Year's Day
February 1, Heroes Day
March 8, Women's Day
March or April, Easter Week
April 7, Genocide Memorial Day
May 1, Labor Day
July 1, Independence Day
August 15, Assumption Day: Catholics celebrate the belief that Mary ascended into heaven after Jesus' death.
November 1, All Saints Day: Catholics celebrate those who have achieved sainthood.
December 25, Christmas: Christians usually attend church and enjoy a special family meal.

Miscellaneous

Pollution – Rwanda at this time does not have any emissions standards. There are very few cars and trucks and factories. Many people burn their trash in the open and the roads can get dusty during the dry season.

Security – Many travel writers in 2013 were saying that Rwanda is one of the safest countries in Africa. Rwanda is not taking chances with problems in Uganda and the Democratic Republic of Congo and soldiers are on hand to protect tourists at almost every turn. The eastern part of the DRC remains volatile and you should remain vigilant. U.S. citizens can visit www.step.state.gov and sign up for the Smart Traveler Program.

Flights to Rwanda - There is only one international airport at the capital city of Kigali. It's an eight-hour flight from Brussels, Belgium. Major airlines flying to Kigali include Rwanda Air Express, Brussels Airlines, Ethiopian Airlines and South Africa Airways. There are also flights to Nairobi where you can then connect to Kigali.

Internet in Rwanda - Now that the Internet is so widespread getting to know the people of Rwanda today is a lot easier than it was when I first visited in 1989. There is all kinds of information online and many of the English speaking people you meet have Internet access and are easy to communicate with. My friend Olivier, who works as a gorilla guide 7 days a week except during the two weeks of the year when he gets a vacation, goes to the Internet Café several times each week. It is great to make a friend in Rwanda and then keep the friendship going when you get home.

I recommend that everyone who goes to Rwanda take the next big step in doing something to help the country. The people who live there are simply wonderful. To write about them and encourage others to get involved is a true blessing.

Most Rwandans do not own cars and have to walk almost everywhere they go.

Dian Fossey

"When you realize the value of all life, you dwell less on what is past and concentrate more on the preservation of the future."

Last entry in Dian Fossey's Journal, 1985

Over the years Dian Fossey has become my conservation hero. At one time I had hoped to meet her, but that hope came to an abrupt end when she was murdered on December 26, 1985.

In working on this book I have been fortunate to meet a number of people who knew Fossey as far back as the early 1970s. My gorilla guide in 1989, who still works in the park today, Francois Bigirimana, was one of her porters. In 2003 I had the great fortune to meet one of her closest friends, Rosamond Carr. I have met some of her former Karisoke staff and a retired government official who knew her from the U.S. Embassy in Kigali. As I assembled the images to complete this book I was fortunate to get to know by email Dr. Alan Goodall who worked with Fossey at Karisoke in 1970.

In May, 2003, Fidele Uwimana, a Field Data Coordinator who works for the Dian Fossey Gorilla Fund International (DFGFI), guided me up the trail to what was left of her Karisoke Research Camp. As a young man Uwimana knew Fossey when he collected wood and water for her. As we climbed the steep and muddy mountain trail to the saddle between Visoke and Karisimbi peaks, Fidele helped me to imagine Fossey's life in the Virungas.

Two hours later we reached the top of the trail and visited the camp and the small little graveyard where Fossey is buried next to some of her favorite gorillas. Nearly everything at the camp was destroyed by rebel soldiers during the genocide and the insecurity that followed. All that remained were the footprints of some of the camp buildings, the gorilla graveyard and the foundation and partial frame of what was a dormitory for the trackers. As I stood under the large Hagenia trees surrounding the camp, I read Fossey's gravestone:

NYIRAMACHABELLI
DIAN FOSSEY 1932-1985
NO ONE LOVED GORILLAS MORE
REST IN PEACE   DEAR FRIEND
ETERNALLY PROTECTED
IN THIS SACRED GROUND
FOR YOU ARE HOME
WHERE YOU BELONG

Nyiramachabelli is Kinyarwandan meaning "lone woman of the forest".

Nearby were the grave sites of some of her beloved gorillas.

Effie 1951-1994
Kazi 1982-1985
Tiger 1967-1987
Nunkie 1956-1985
Kweli 1975-1978
Uncle Bert 1952-1978
Digit 1965-1977

Visiting the place where Fossey spent so many years studying and protecting the gorillas made for an unforgettable day. I not only could imagine her walking around the camp with her dog Cindy and pet monkey Kima; I could smell the mountain air and store the memory of her camp and forest surroundings deep within my mind forever.

My good fortune continued during the summer of 2006 when I was invited to speak about the park and the gorillas at the Las Cruces Museum of Natural History in New Mexico. Little did I know that someone who knew Fossey during her last years living in the Virungas was in the audience and lived so close to my home in El Paso, Texas. Judy Chidester, a friend of Fossey and a resident of nearby Las Cruces, New Mexico provided me with a special interview.

In late 2012 when working on a revised version of this book, I was able to spend time visiting with Joseph Munyaneza, one of the last persons to see Dian Fossey before she was found murdered on December 27, 1985. Joseph was the first Rwandan graduate student to study under Fossey. On December 22 of that year in a letter Fossey wrote to Rosamond Carr she referred to him as "my wonderful Rwandan student." While at Karisoke he studied the insects of the Hagenia forest. He had dinner with her and Wayne McGuire, an American researcher, on Christmas Eve. He said that she gave him a calculator and that he would never forget her kindness. Someday I may share more of my interview. He was very close to her and can still picture her 27 years later.

Crowned Crane.

Dian Fossey

Dian Fossey was born in San Francisco, California on January 16, 1932. She graduated from San Jose State College in 1954 with a degree in occupational therapy. Less than a year after graduation she moved to Louisville, Kentucky to pursue a career working at the Korsair Children's Hospital as Director of the Occupational Therapy Department.

As a child Fossey often dreamed of going to Africa, a goal that she started to seriously plan for in 1960. Three years later on September 23, 1963, after taking out an $8,000 loan, she was on her way to East Africa. In preparing for her trip she read every book about Africa she could get her hands on including a copy of George Schaller's book, *The Year of the Gorilla*. She was inspired by Schaller's mountain gorilla research from his 1959 study in the Virungas. Little did she know that four years later she would find herself continuing Schaller's research in the same Kabara Meadow where he and his wife came to know one of the world's most amazing primates.

Fossey is known around the world as the person most responsible for saving the mountain gorilla from extinction. Many first heard of Fossey's efforts about the same time the western world was experiencing a renewed spirit to reconnect with nature. National Geographic's January 1970 issue pictured Fossey on the cover with two orphaned baby mountain gorillas. It was published just a few months prior to the first Earth Day celebration in the U.S.

On her first visit Fossey was guided into the park by renowned filmmakers, Joan and Alan Root. Thanks to Dr. Leakey's support, three years later in December, 1966, arrangements were made for Fossey to return to Africa to begin her monumental research project at Kabara Meadow.

Fossey's work in Kabara was cut short when she was forced to leave the mountains during a rebellion in the Province of Zaire (now called the Democratic Republic of Congo, DRC). After a close call with the rebels, she reluctantly moved to the Rwanda side of the Virungas and established a new camp. Karisoke became her research headquarters on September 24, 1967 at 4:30pm. In her book, *Gorillas in the Mist*, Fossey described how she came up with the name Karisoke: "Kari" for the first four letters of Mt. Karisimbi that overlooked the camp and "the "soke" for the last four letters of Mt. Visoke, whose slopes rose north some 12,172 feet immediately behind the 10,000 foot campsite".

From 1967 to the last day of her life in 1985, Fossey was totally dedicated to research, conservation and protection of the estimated population of 242 (1981 census) mountain gorillas living in the Virungas. Thanks to her steadfastness, courage and passion, central Africa's conservation movement was raised another notch. Today the movement remains vibrant and strong as governments expand conservation activities, international organizations help develop important conservation strategies and African

Dian Fossey with her porters as she leaves for Cambridge University on August 13, 1970.

institutions of higher learning facilitate the training of students to fill important conservation positions.

Fossey may not be remembered as the world's first dedicated primatologist, but she will always be remembered as one of the world's first die-hard wildlife warriors. Some of the most influential and passionate wildlife advocates working around the globe today have been influenced by her work. Since Fossey's death in 1985, many have helped to keep her torch aglow by dedicating their lives to help to protect the gorillas. Gorilla conservationists, educators and conservation organizations around the world continue to support her research and conservation efforts. Few conservation projects anywhere can compare. All of the successes, past and present, and the challenges to be faced in the future, shine as a beacon of hope for conservation everywhere.

When Steve Irwin, wildlife advocate and Australia's most famous ambassador for conservation, died in 2006, many lamented his loss. Some put him in the same category with Dian Fossey, Jane Goodall and Sir David Attenborough. It is a tremendous credit to Fossey and testimony to her enduring contributions that her name will long be remembered as a symbol of wildlife conservation.

Fossey's life and research is best chronicled in her book *Gorillas in the Mist* published in 1983. Following her death, Farley Mowat, a Canadian author and conservationist, wrote a biography, *Woman in the Mists: The Story of Dian Fossey*. His work included extensive excerpts from her personal journal and archives. No other publication, outside of Fossey's own book, offers such an in-depth look at how she struggled to maintain her research efforts and sanity while dealing with poachers and the many characters she encountered including government officials, students, friends and lovers, African staff, media and tourists.

The National Geographic photographer who took the 1970 cover photo of Fossey along with thousands of other images and hundreds of hours of film footage was Bob Campbell. He was portrayed as a main character and Fossey's lover in the movie *Gorillas in the Mist*, a relationship that eventually went sour. Many suspect that as a result, Fossey gave him little credit for his efforts in helping to habituate the gorillas when her book was published in 1983.

Seventeen years later Campbell published his own book, *The Taming of the Gorillas* (Minerva Press LTD, 2000), where he tells his story of Fossey and the gorillas including how he played a role in helping her get closer to the gorillas while working to get great photographs and video footage. Unfortunately *The Taming of the Gorillas* is out of print and finding a library copy is very difficult.

Another attempt to tell Campbell's story is included in the National Geographic documentary, *The Lost Film of Dian Fossey*. The film features interviews with Campbell and footage that National Geographic had lost track of for nearly thirty years. After several years of trying I finally obtained a copy of the film from a 2003 television broadcast in Australia. In the film Campbell talks candidly about his relationship with Fossey and there are incredible scenes of the two orphaned babies Coco and Pucker playing with her dog Cindy before the two were taken to the Cologne Zoo. Hopefully, someday American viewers will have an opportunity to see this film especially in light of the 40th anniversary of the establishment of Karisoke in 2007 and the 2009 Year of the

Gorilla recognition officially launched on December 2, 2008 by the U.N.-backed Convention on the Conservation of Migratory Species of Wild Animals.

Many of Fossey's letters, journal entries and rare photographs, taken by Fossey and Bob Campbell, have been published in a large format book called *No One Loved Gorillas More*. Fossey's life has been chronicled in numerous ways by many people, but very little has been recorded by Rwandans themselves outside of news reports published since her death. One of the best insights into how the people of Rwanda felt about her was provided in an interview Rosamond Carr gave Georgianne Nienaber in 2005. When asked how she thought Fossey is remembered in Rwanda, Carr said that "the people who really knew Dian remember her for her generosity." She told the story of how her long-time employee Sembagare, upon meeting Fossey as she drove her Land Rover "Lily" down the road, told her that his wife was about to have a baby and needed to walk twenty miles to the hospital. "Dian immediately offered him the keys to the Land Rover and told him to hurry to the hospital. Sembagare will never forget that moment." Carr also made a point of saying that Fossey was "loved by many people and was a prolific correspondent."

When I met Rosamond Carr in 2003 at her lake side home on Lake Kivu at Rubavu, we spoke mainly about her work at the Imbabazi orphanage she started in late 1994 for orphans of the genocide. I was so honored to have the opportunity to meet one of the greatest American ladies Rwanda has ever known. At the time the orphanage was operating out of an old hotel. However, in late 2005 she was able to move the children back to a new, permanent location at her farm at Mugongo. Carr died of pneumonia at her home at the age of 94 on September 29, 2006. Her autobiography, *Land of a Thousand Hills*, is a must read for anyone interested in learning more about Rwanda. For more information on the orphanage and/or to send a contribution visit www.imbabazi.org or write:

Imbabazi Orphanage
c/o Ann H. Roehrs
546 Gramercy Lane
Downingtown, PA 19335

Ros Carr in her beloved flower plantation at Mugongo near Gisenyi.

The respect and admiration Rwandans had and still have today for Dian Fossey is clearly expressed in a government cable that was released to the public. The following communication, released and unclassified by the United States Department of State on December 20, 2006, was sent as a cable from the American Embassy in Kigali to the Secretary of State in Washington D.C. on January 2, 1986 a week following Fossey's tragic death:

1. A delegation from the Office Rwandaise de Tourisme et Parcs Nationales, headed by Director Laurent Habiyaremye, called on the charge, Emerson MeLaven, the morning of January 2, 1986 to express their official condolences on the death of Dr. Dian Fossey. Their prepared remarks are quoted below.

2. "Ladies, Gentlemen, Militants and supporters of M.R.N.D: It was with great sorrow that the Trustees, the Board of Directors and the personnel of the Rwandan Board of Tourism and

Dian Fossey

National Parks learned of the death of Dr. Dian Fossey while working in the National Volcano Park. Dr. Dian Fossey was murdered during the night of December 26 to December 27, 1985 at the Karisoke Research Station which she, herself, created in 1967. An eminent scientist of international renown, Dr. Dian Fossey remains the person to have made the greatest contribution towards the protection of the mountain gorilla (Gorilla gorilla beringei), a rare species in danger of extinction, now found only in our range of volcanoes.

For the past 18 years, she has defied the jealous and discouraged wrongdoers in order to bring the entire world to finally understand the importance of protecting the National Volcano Park, privileged habitat of this Anthropoid, our distant ancestor.

Poaching was considerably and noticeably overcome thanks to her on-the-spot interventions as well as through international opinion. It is to this that Rwanda owes its reputation as a champion of conservation.

Dr. Dian Fossey was also the creator of a selective form of tourism based on the visiting of groups of gorillas accustomed to the presence of humans according to scientific data which she gave in keeping with this species.

Scientists and research workers from all corners of the world found in her a devoted and unselfish person whose principal concern was the survival of humanity in an ecologically balanced world.

The fact that she specified before her death that she wished to be buried beside these primates is sufficient proof of her attachment to our country. The Rwandan Board of Tourism and National Parks recognizes that she did not deserve what happened to her that night; but she should know, where she is resting now for eternity, that she is still alive in the hearts of the Board and the Karisoke Research Station."

It is interesting to read the comment about the "selective form of tourism." Fossey was well known for her opposition to tourists visiting the gorillas. In a cable to her family in California the following was hand delivered to Mr. and Mrs. Richard Price:

From the American Embassy, Kigali, Rwanda:

The Government of Rwanda has asked us to express its shock and deep sympathy of all Rwandans over the death of your daughter Dian. They wished us to convey to you that they feel that Dian was a part of Rwanda and that what she has accomplished here will live on.

Dian leaving her cabin (on right) to meet the porters who are waiting in line with their loads at their feet by the camp fire.

The only other person I was able to interview who spent any time with Fossey was a wonderful lady I met in 2006. Judy Chidester invited me to her home and told me the story of how in February, 1980 she was able to spend a week at Karisoke taking care of a little orphan gorilla. When Fossey was getting ready to leave the country to work on her book at Cornell University, Chidester was able to help Fossey take care of a baby mountain gorilla that had been taken from Zairoise (DRC) poachers.

On New Year's Day, 1980, poachers tried to sell the baby to a doctor in Musanze. The baby was soon turned over to Fossey who later named her Bonne Annee (Happy New Year). Four months later the little gorilla was successfully reintroduced into the forest. For a year Bonnee Annee was an important part of Peanut's Group until she died in May, 1981 from pneumonia. To this day she represents the only mountain gorilla to be successfully returned to the wild.

Judy Chidester on November 28, 2008 holding a picture of her and Bonne Annee at Karisoke.

Chidester worked in Rwanda as a communications program officer at the Embassy of the United States in Kigali from 1976-81. She recalls speaking to Fossey long into the night at Fossey's home in Kigali. Although Fossey had a reputation for being very strong willed and some people had a hard time communicating with her, Chidester said that she "could see her dedication and humanness" and "realized that beneath a brittle exterior she was a very wonderful person". She respected Fossey and when she wrote an article about her experience at Karisoke for the *Department of State Newsletter*, she asked Fossey to review it before it was published.

When recalling the week she slept in Dian's cabin, Chidester remembers how up until that time she "had never been cold in Rwanda." Fossey's cabin was "made out of corrugated metal" and her "bed had sheets, two or three blankets and two layers of sleeping bags." It was so cold that when she went to bed she needed two hot water bottles, "one behind my knees and one in my arms, it was so cold."

Bonnee Annee was having some health problems (diarrhea) and Dian had a little sleeping box constructed in her room. Interestingly, Chidester related that "a young African fellow would come in every night to make a new nest of branches in the gorilla nest box in the bedroom. At that point we thought it was a male called Charlie. He would wake up before I was ready to get up and I learned to make gorilla vocalizations and he would be quiet." Later it was learned that Charlie was a female and was renamed Bonnee Annee.

When Chidester got up to take care of the baby she would put on a poncho and let the little gorilla down from the cage. It was obvious that the gorilla wanted to be hugged. Chidester wore the poncho because the baby was covered with urine. The baby would then reach inside the poncho, so as Chidester reasoned, to feel her warm flesh.

Every day she gave the baby gorilla medicine with berries and would take her (she wanted to be carried) and Dian's dog Cindy out for a walk. The April 1980 issue of the Department of State Newsletter featured a two page article Chidester wrote about her experience. Her story is too precious not to include here in its entirety.

"Six days with Charlie were among the most memorable in my life." Judy Chidester.

Getting to know a gorilla...
Charlie was a girl and real cuddly

By Judy A. Chidester

Kigali, Rwanda –When I joined the Foreign Service, 20 years ago, I hoped, as most people do, for an interesting, adventurous life. I haven't been disappointed. I saw part of the filming of "Lawrence of Arabia". I visited such remote and interesting sites as the ruins of Petra, in southwest Jordan. I toured the river temples in Thailand, and the Amazon River and Iguassu

Falls in Brazil. I survived the first embassy bombing in Vietnam. But recently I had an experience that overshadows all the others — I was a babysitter for a gorilla.

The three-year old ape — a girl gorilla named Charlie — belongs to Dian Fossey, a primatologist, who maintains a study camp on a volcanic mountain about a three-hour drive from the embassy. Ms. Fossey had to come to the capital city on business, and she asked Rick Kramer, our administrative officer, if someone could come to the mountain to take care of Charlie. Happily, Mr. Kramer thought of me, and off I went.

After a rough trip over bumpy, mucky roads, the driver let me off at the bottom of Mount Visoke, at 8,000 feet. Ms. Fossey's porters were waiting. They loaded my cooler of food and my suitcase on their heads, and we began a two-hour climb up the mountain to the site, at 10,000 feet. About half-way up, one of the porters led to where I could see the main study group of gorillas, on the hillside above us, I could easily distinguish the Silverback, or dominant male, as the apes foraged for food. We then proceeded to Ms. Fossey's cabin, where I would stay. This was where I met my young charge. Charlie was about three feet tall and weighed 28-30 lbs. Ms. Fossey was still there and, before her departure, she gave me instructions on how to handle Charlie. She departed the next morning; leaving me and Peter Veit, a student, in camp with her African staff. Mr. Veit's duties took him out of camp daily from about 8:30am to 4 p.m.

Meanwhile, I attempted to play mother to the little gorilla. Charlie was extremely affectionate and dependent, with no tendency at all to stray from my side. One of Ms. Fossey's employees gathered food for Charlie several times a day. She ate it readily, but seemed to relish even more what she found herself on our little jaunts.

After each little trek of approximately 45 minutes came a nap period. Charlie would curl up around me, and usually sitting or lying on my lap, facing me, with her arms around me or with her hands clasped under her head in a very human-like position. Needless to say, diapers weren't part of the deal — so I found that putting a waterproof poncho over my lap while holding her made the rest of my day more comfortable. But this didn't please Charlie very much. Body contact seemed very important to her, and she devised various methods to try to push the poncho off my lap or to get me to move it.

Charlie's rest periods were about the only times that I could relax and read. At other times, Charlie would knock the book out of my hand, and, often, try to eat it. After the naps, she was full of vim and vigor and wanted to explore and feed again. She was receiving medication for a diarrhea problem three times a day, and Vitamin C once a day. Luckily, she liked both medicines, and looked forward to them and the treat of berries that followed.

Each day as darkness fell, one of the employees brought in moss for the bottom of Charlie's sleeping nest – a sort of cage on the wall, about six feet from the floor. After he spread the moss, he brought in stalks of a tree-like plant which I broke and laid in the nest in true gorilla fashion, as Ms. Fossey had shown me. She was trying to hold Charlie to the same feeding and sleeping habits and conditions as she would have had in the wild, and was hoping to re-introduce Charlie, eventually, to one of the groups of gorillas that live on the mountain. After the nest was ready, I would put a small plastic container, holding some cookies and fruit, inside. Later she counted on it, and would climb up from time to time to see if it was there yet.

I found that, if we took several long walks a day, Charlie's eyelids would droop like a little child's by about 6:45pm., and that all she would want to do was cuddle. At these indications, I would give her the last dose of medicine and urge her into bed. She would go willingly, and I would sit with her for 15 to 20 minutes while she munched her treats and settled herself in for the night. After this, her food provider would sit with her until she dozed off.

During my stay I learned a new skill –belch vocalizing. Belch vocalizations (a sort of "MMM-MOAMMM" sound) are made by gorillas when they're content, especially while enjoying something they're eating. There is also the "pig grunt" (yes, that's what it sounds like) that indicates displeasure. Reinforcing Charlie's use of these sounds, and joining her in making them, are extremely important, as she will need them when she re-enters the world of the wild and encounters others of her own kind.

In the evenings, Mr. Veit usually joined me for a simple meal and some human conversation by the fire. When he would return to his own cabin to prepare his daily notes, I was more than ready to crawl into my own heavily-covered bed and snuggle up to a hot water bottle, usually by 9 p.m.

These six days with Charlie were among the most memorable in my life. A young gorilla is an extremely intelligent animal, and its day-by-day reactions to discoveries are interesting to watch. As an example, after a hailstorm one day, Charlie scooped up a handful of hailstones, wondering whether they were a new treat. The quizzical look on her wrinkled young face was priceless; it was one of the many things I'd have enjoyed sharing with others.

On my third night at camp, Elizabeth Escher, a Swiss friend, came up to lend a hand and to take pictures. The accompanying photographs are hers.

I can't imagine Foreign Service life ever becoming boring.

Dian Fossey and the US Ambassador to Rwanda, Robert Melone, with Charlie (Bonne Annee) at Karisoke.

In looking back at her Karisoke experience twenty-six years later Chidester said that when she was there she "realized that if I was Dian Fossey, I would have stayed up there too. It was a totally peaceful time, and I did not have to worry about safety. I felt so lucky to have had the opportunity to spend time up there. I felt very fortunate to have had a relationship with a wild animal."

The Karisoke Research Center is now operated by the Dian Fossey Gorilla Fund International (DFGFI) in cooperation with the Government of Rwanda. The center was reestablished in the town of Musanze after the original buildings and facilities were destroyed by rebels during the genocide.

Mountain gorilla research is critical to saving the Virunga ecosystem. The overall well-being of the world's biodiversity is enhanced by how well ecosystems function and how their components remain intact. Healthy ecosystems are critical to our survival, not just where we live, but all around the world. How well these systems function is important to the animals and plants that help to hold them together.

The gorilla's ecosystem contribution is a prime example of the way people benefit from a wide variety of ecosystem services. Those services include oxygen production, carbon dioxide assimilation, pollination, fresh water systems and genetic diversity important to agriculture, soil resources and all the benefits afforded by the world's biodiversity. Food and new medicines derived from delicate ecosystems help to exemplify the gorilla's role.

Karisoke's contributions to the further understanding of the gorilla population and their place in the mountain environment are significant. The primatologist community credits Fossey for her research on mountain gorilla behavior and socioecology, including infant development, ranging, migration/transfers, vocalizations, feeding ecology, reproduction, infanticide and population dynamics including census work and demography. Since 1967 over fifty other researchers have continued her work adding considerably to the world's understanding of the mountain gorilla.

To help others keep up with gorilla research activities in the Virungas DFGFI regularly publishes "Field News" reports at www.gorillafund.org. Membership privileges afford additional news reports including opportunities to attend DFGFI sponsored events.

To commemorate 40 years of mountain gorilla research since Fossey began her mountain gorilla research in 1967, DFGFI has begun a project to digitize Dian Fossey documents and research reports. Working in cooperation with the Rwandan government and many conservation organizations and Fossey colleagues, Rwandan University Students were asked to help with the project that will eventually make the entire archive available on the Internet.

DFGFI is helping to keep Fossey's legacy alive in a myriad of ways. The organization has three major goals:

1. Conservation and protection of gorillas and their habitat in Africa

2. Promoting continued research on their threatened ecosystems and education about their relevance to the world in which we live.

3. Providing assistance to local communities through education, training and economic development initiatives.

DFGFI is also working in the DRC where nearly 50% of the mountain gorilla population lives in the Virunga National Park. In addition, an extensive field program conducted largely by Africans includes community-based preserves and national parks established to protect nearly the entire range of the eastern lowland gorilla. In both Rwanda and the DRC the organization also sponsors other important health and community development programs.

The European counterpart organization to DFGFI, recently renamed the Gorilla Organization, also includes news reports on mountain gorillas at www.gorillas.org.

More Internet Resources

Rwanda Development Board (RDB), www.rwandatourism.com

For news and information about Volcanoes National Park and other ecotourism opportunities in Rwanda the RDB site is updated on a regular basis.

Gorilla Journal, www.berggorilla.de

To learn more about gorilla conservation across Africa including news and information about the five subspecies of eastern and western gorillas, Berggorilla & Regenwald Direkthilfe maintain a highly informative website available in English, French and German. It includes copies of newsletters published since 2000.

Official Website of Virunga National Park, www.virunga.org

A newly launched website blog at virunga.org was announced during the summer of 2008. The site includes updates on mountain gorilla conservation news and activities on the DRC side of the international protected area at Virunga National Park. Since gorillas at Volcanoes National Park often cross over into the DRC, this website is of particular interest to people following news of gorillas they have seen or know about in Rwanda. In early 2007 a Congo Institute for Nature Conservation (ICCN) park warden posted news from Virunga National Park on the wildlifedirect.org blog site before the creation of virunga.org. His reports detailed efforts to monitor and protect three gorilla groups in the Bukima area where National Congress for the Defense of the People (CNDP) rebels would eventually take over the Mikeno Gorilla Sector. The death of the silverback Senkekwe, the leader of the Rugendo family along with three other family members, helped to draw international attention to the ongoing carnage at Virungas National Park where hundreds of hippos were reported killed the year before.

The best way to understand Fossey and her work is to read her book *Gorillas in the Mist*. The book chronicles her research efforts from 1967 to 1983. Illustrations include graphs, line drawings and 53 black and white photographs, many of them taken by Fossey. There are chapters describing her first year at Kabara Meadow, an extensive description of the social life of Group Five, how she cared for orphan gorillas taken from poachers, wildlife other than gorillas living near Karisoke Research Centre, the impact of poachers and the formation of a new gorilla family. The Appendix includes a list of plants eaten by gorillas, population statistics, information on gorilla vocalizations and parasites and 13 pages detailing the results of the autopsies of 14 gorillas, including the famous male gorilla Digit, who was killed by poachers.

Few of the gorillas that Fossey knew and studied are alive today. Pablo's Group and Beetsme's Group are two groups that DFGFI staff have monitored over the years from the Karisoke Research Center. Each group is named after the dominant or once dominant silverback leader of the group. The groups are always changing and the DFGFI website at www.gorillafund.org includes updates on changes to each group.

The constant changes in the gorilla groups make it difficult for the general public to keep up. The following summarizes the makeup of some of the research groups from 2008 to 2015.

Pablo's Group

A portion of the group Fossey called Group Five is now called Pablo's Group. The well known gorilla Pablo was once the group's dominant silverback. Fossey was very fond of Pablo who in some early films, as a three year old, is shown approaching her in a playful manner. Group Five was one of Fossey's main study groups and was the

Lone silverback Nyakarima.

group that Sigourney Weaver spent most of her time with during the two month period that she was with the gorillas filming the movie *Gorillas in the Mist*. Group 5 split in 1993 into two groups: Shinda and Pablo's groups. Pablo was last seen on July 13, 2008 when he left the group with another silverback. DFGFI announced in their fall newsletter that he was presumed dead.

In late 2008 the dominant silverback of Pablo's group was Cantsbee. Fossey named this gorilla, who is the son of Puck, when he was born on November 14, 1978. She was always amazed by Puck's behavior and was unaware that Puck was pregnant when she gave birth and was informed of the event by one of her students. In learning of the birth Fossey exclaimed "It can't be!" She then named the 1978 surprise baby "Cantsbee." When I started working on this book in 2005 Pablo's group was the largest group known from the Virungas with 61 individuals. At one time the group actually reached 65 individuals. However, in 2006 researchers were seeing signs that the group was about to split. By December 16, 2014 the group size had decreased to 30. Cantsbee turned 35 years old on November 14, 2013.

Beetsme's Group

Beetsme was named by Fossey in November, 1975 when he was found traveling as a young male in Group Eight with Peanuts, the son of Rafiki. Fossey described Rafiki as the "regal monarch of the mountain". He died of pneumonia and pleurisy in 1974. Beetsme was first observed by Fossey in 1975. She was surprised to find out that he was a male when he joined another group. Up until that time she had never seen a blackback male join a strange group and said to herself "beats me!" Beetsme eventually became the dominant silverback until he began sharing leadership with the silverback Titus. Beetsme died when he was about 36 years old in 2001. The group split in 2007 and was led by the silverback Titus until he died on September 14, 2009.

Shinda's Group

Shinda used to be a member of Group Five where he was born to Marchessa on the evening of February 27, 1977. Shinda is an African word meaning "overcome". He was very fragile when he was born. He was the dominant silverback up until he died of natural causes on November 24, 2008. The group split with some members following Ugenda and others following Ntambara.

To learn even more and better understand Fossey, you can also watch video interviews she gave National Geographic, PBS, BBC and Mutual of Omaha's Wild Kingdom. Some of these productions are still available online. Mutual of Omaha's Wild Kingdom *The African Wild* DVD set is a three disc collection that features ten episodes focused on gorillas, elephants, giraffes, hippopotami, lions, cheetah and other fauna of Africa. Among the standout scenes, *Reunion with the Gorillas*, was aired in 1984 and features Fossey reuniting with her gorillas after a three year absence teaching at Cornell University and finishing her book *Gorillas in the Mist*. The episode shows Group Five with Beethoven and Fossey playing a tickling game with Puck. Before she finds Group Five she first comes across Nunkie's Group, Peanut's (bachelor) Group and a lone male named Tiger. When she finds Group Five and its silverback Beethoven, contact is soon made with most of the thirteen gorillas in the group. A juvenile touches her and she is obviously accepted. The playfulness of the young gorilla Puck as he approaches her with his younger sister is testimony to Fossey's amazing relationship with the gorillas.

Fossey worked to protect her beloved gorillas up until her death in 1985. Her murderer has never been found, but her efforts live on. In the intervening decades hundreds of dedicated park guards, trackers, biologists, conservationists have worked diligently to protect the mountain gorillas in their last remaining habitat. They have been supported by thousands of concerned citizens from around the world who have donated towards research and conservation programs and have paid up to $750 for a park permit to see gorillas in the wild.

Dian Fossey Chronology

January 16, 1932: born in San Francisco, California.

1949: Graduates from High School, studies business at Martin Junior College.

1954: Graduates from San Jose State College with a B.A. in Occupational Therapy.

1954: Becomes Director of Occupational Therapy, Kosair Children's Hospital, Louisville, Kentucky.

1963: Travels to Africa to meet Dr. Louis Leaky and see the mountain gorillas.

May, 1966: Dr. Louis Leaky approves her request to carry out research on mountain gorillas.

December 15, 1966: Departs U.S. for Africa.

December, 1966: Begins field study at Kabara, in the Democratic Republic of Congo.

January 19, 1967: First real contact (3 hours) with a family of nine gorillas in Kabara – Group 1.

July 9, 1967: Congolese Civil War. Soldiers force Fossey to leave Kabara.

September 24, 1967: Establishes new research camp at Karisoke.

December 31, 1967: Fossey surpasses Schaller hours of observation mark by accumulating 485 hours of time observing the gorillas.

September, 1968: National Geographic Photographer Robert Campbell arrives at Karisoke.

September, 1968: Fossey returns to the U.S. for the first time in two years to attend the funeral of her father who had committed suicide.

May 3, 1969: Baby gorillas Coco and Pucker leave Kigali Airport for the Cologne Zoo, Germany.

November, 1969: Fossey hikes to Kabara Meadow and discovers that fewer than half of the gorillas she had known in the area from 1967 still survived.

November 17, 1969: Fossey is bitten by a poacher's dog and soon enters a hospital in Musanze. She returns to camp on December 30 after recuperating at Roz Carr's plantation.

January, 1970: National Geographic Magazine publishes cover article by Fossey detailing the first three years of her research.

January 11, 1970: Fossey begins her first three-month term towards her doctorate at Cambridge University.

April, 1970: Fossey returns to Karisoke.

September, 1970: Fossey returns to Cambridge leaving Alan Goodall in charge of Karisoke.

March 12, 1971: Fossey returns to Karisoke.

October, 1971: National Geographic publishes Fossey's second article on the gorillas.

1972: There were ninety-six gorillas in eight groups living in or on the fringes of Karisoke study area. Dian begins to grow close to gorilla in Group 4 including Digit.

February, 1972: Munyarukiko, a Twa poacher, was captured and escorted to jail in Musanze.

May 29, 1972: Bob Campbell leaves Karisoke for the last time.

Summer, 1973: Kelly Stewart, daughter of actor James Stewart, arrives to begin research project at Karisoke.

October, 1973: Fossey leaves for a lecture tour in the United States featuring a newly completed National Geographic film about the gorillas.

January, 1974: Fossey returns to Cambridge for final four months of study.

May 6, 1974: Fossey returns to Karisoke.

May, 1976: Fossey returns to Cambridge for oral exam and receives her doctorate.

1976: A doctor in Musanze tells Fossey that thirty-six gorilla heads were brought into town to be sold as souvenirs.

May, 1977: Film crew arrives at Karisoke to make a documentary about Fossey and the gorillas for the television series *Wild Kingdom*.

December 31, 1977: Fossey's favorite gorilla, Digit, is killed by poachers while defending his family in Group Four.

January 1, 1978: David Attenborough and BBC film unit visited Karisoke for the television series *Life on Earth*.

February 3, 1978: One of the world's most celebrated TV anchors, Walter Cronkite of CBS News, announces the death of Digit.

July 24, 1978: Uncle Bert, who had taken control of Group Four when Digit was shot, is shot and killed by poachers.

1978: Coco and Pucker die within one month of each other at the Cologne Zoo

March 3, 1980: Fossey leaves Rwanda for Cornell University in New York to begin a teaching assignment and write her book, *Gorillas in the Mist*.

March 21, 1980: The baby gorilla Bonne Annee was successfully reintroduced into the wild into Group Four led by Peanuts.

September 6, 1983: Fossey attends Explorer's Club publicity event in the United States to promote the publishing of her book, *Gorillas in the Mist*.

November 22, 1983: Fossey returns to Rwanda.

Dian Fossey

October 27, 1984: Fossey presented with the Joseph Wood Krutch Medal at the Humane Society's annual convention in San Diego, California.

April, 1985: Fossey signs contract with Universal Studios for a movie to be based on her book, *Gorillas in the Mist*.

June 19, 1985: Fossey appears as a guest on the *Tonight Show* with Johnny Carson.

September 11, 1985: 60th Anniversary of the establishment of the original Albert National Park.

October, 1985: For the first time the local media showed a real interest in Fossey's work when all three Rwanda newspapers send reporters and photographers to do stories.

December 3, 1985: After a series of frustrating problems getting her work Visa renewed Fossey is given a special visa authorizing her to stay in Rwanda for two years.

December 22, 1985: Fossey's last letter to her best friend Rosamond Carr thanks her for her the Christmas gift that she received on that day. The letter is never finished. At the bottom of the last page of her journal, carefully printed in block letters are the following words: When you realize the value of all life, you dwell less on what is past and concentrate more on the preservation of the future.

December 27, 1985: Fossey is found murdered at her Karisoke cabin.

"In a world older and more complete than ours, they move finished and complete, gifted with extensions of the senses we have lost or never attained, living by voices we shall never hear. They are not brethren; they are not underlings; they are other nations, caught with ourselves in the net of life and time, fellow prisoners of the splendor and travail of the earth."

Henry Beston, The Outermost House, 1928

I shall never forget the day I first laid eyes on a family of mountain gorillas. It was February 3, 1989 on a visit to see Group 11 at Volcanoes National Park. I had joined an East African bird watching safari on a two-week journey across Kenya and Rwanda. I like bird watching, but my main reason for joining the group was the opportunity to see the gorillas. My videotape of that day helps me to remember almost every moment.

As we approached a high ridge overlooking what was then called Zaire (DRC) our guide took us over to a small patch of trees. There, in great anticipation, a lifelong dream was finally coming true. My first wild gorilla was high in a tree. We had walked almost two hours through bamboo forest and thick vegetation. I imagined seeing a gorilla around almost every bend. At last the moment had arrived. First I saw movement in the shadows. Soon a female and her baby came into view as they climbed down to where we could get a better look. The rest of the group appeared moments later including a silverback named Stilgar and his next in line rival, Ndume.

I was completely caught off guard at how close we had approached. The gorillas were all around us and acted as if we were just another part of the natural landscape. I sensed no fear from the gorillas, just a little anticipation from members of my human group as the large black creatures walked by, interacting only with each other. During the hour that we spent in the shade of that little patch of trees the gorillas simply carried on eating, resting and playing. As our guide tried to communicate with the few English words in his vocabulary, he pointed out two silverbacks and called out "chief, chief".

One silverback broke off a tree limb and with a branch in hand ran by the other as if to say "hey look at me, watch out!" Another ran by beating his chest. Suddenly we heard loud screams coming from the trees across the way. It sounded like a family fight. After about a minute of listening to loud screaming vocalizations two large black backs appeared out of the shadows and once again there was calm. As I watched the amazing family scene unfold, I kept thinking about how observing wild gorillas might compare to how life looked for a family of early humans.

Today I find myself spending more and more of my time worrying about their fate. I also think about all the hate in the world and how people are killing each other in wars and in all kinds of other violent acts. Then I think back on the gorillas in the Virungas and how although their numbers have increased in recent years, their existence remains threatened by poachers, political unrest and diseases like Ebola. And I am reminded of Beston's reflections on life, and in a small way I am comforted. The gorillas, magnificently designed to survive in a high elevation rainforest, are "other nations, caught with ourselves in the net of life and time, fellow prisoners of the splendor and travail of the earth." Like I wish for my own kind, I wish the gorillas well.

Mother mountain gorilla with baby.

The Mountain Gorillas

Most people think of one kind of gorilla, the one you see in a zoo or on a television nature program. Zoos and documentaries made for television have helped many to know and better understand the world of gorillas, but not everyone reads zoo graphics or watches nature programs. No other species of gorilla has been studied in as much detail as the mountain gorilla. Impressive arrays of research papers and monographs have been published and with the current threats to gorillas from habitat loss and from poaching, research activities will continue to support conservation strategies for years to come.

The Mountain Gorillas

Taxonomists currently recognize two species of gorillas split into four to five subspecies. In the far eastern edge of Central Africa there is the mountain gorilla (*Gorilla beringei beringei*) living in the Virungas of Rwanda, DRC and Uganda. Approximately 20 miles to the north in Uganda there is the Bwindi gorilla (*Gorilla beringei spp.*) of Bwindi Impenetrable National Park. Although the taxonomic status of the Bwindi gorilla is debated by some primatologists, the International Union for the Conservation of Nature lumps the Virunga and Bwindi populations as one, *Gorilla beringei*. As a result, many combine the two populations calling them all mountain gorillas. This explains why some say that there are fewer than 500 mountain gorillas while others say around 880. A gorilla census conducted at Bwindi in 2012 estimated 400 gorillas, up from 302 counted in 2006. Dr. Alecia Lilly, who was Vice President of Africa Programs for DFGFI before she died in 2009, believed that taxonomists will eventually agree that the gorillas living in the Virungas are distinct from those at Bwindi.

Grauer's Gorilla, Chimanuka, at Kahuzi-Biega National Park, Bukavu, Democratic Republic of Congo.

Another subspecies, the Grauer's gorilla (*Gorilla beringei graueri*) lives north and west of the Virungas in eastern DRC. One population of Grauer's lives about 25 miles (40 km) northwest of Musanze in DRC's Maiko National Park.

In the western part of Central Africa there are two recognized subspecies. The western lowland gorilla (*Gorilla gorilla gorilla*) lives in the lowland tropical forests of southern Cameroon, the southwest corner of the Central African Republic, Republic of Congo, Equatorial Guinea, Gabon and southwards towards the Cabinda enclave of Angola. The newly discovered Cross River gorilla (*Gorilla gorilla deihli*) lives in a small border region of Nigeria and Cameroon.

More people are familiar with the western lowland gorilla, the commonly seen species in zoos. Currently the estimated captive population in major zoos around the world is estimated to be over 776 gorillas. In 2014 the only other gorilla species held in a zoo anywhere was the Grauer's gorilla at the Antwerp Zoo in Belgium where they had one female.

The rarest of the five subspecies is the Cross River Gorilla. In 2014 the total population was estimated to be 295 gorillas living in eleven groups. The second rarest, depending on whether you recognize two subspecies or one, is the Bwindi gorilla or the mountain gorilla. All species of gorilla are listed by the International Union for the Conservation of Nature (IUCN) as endangered. The mountain gorilla, Bwindi gorilla and Cross River gorilla and western lowland are listed by IUCN as critically endangered. Critically endangered species are those that face an extremely high risk of extinction in the immediate future. Immediate future means that the population numbers are low enough to risk that the species could go extinct within a period of 5-10 years.

The most widespread subspecies is the western lowland gorilla. Even though they are not as rare as other subspecies, all is not well for westerns. It is estimated that over 50% of the population was lost in recent years from poaching and diseases like Ebola. In 2007 the population was estimated by some to be at about 35,000. A year later the estimate jumped by 125,000 when the Wildlife Conservation Society announced the discovery of a previously unknown high density of western gorillas living in a remote region of the Republic of Congo. In 2014 WCS estimated a total wild population of 150,000 with numbers steadily declining.

Silverback western lowland gorilla at the Albuquerque Zoo in New Mexico.

    The second most abundant subspecies is the Grauer's gorilla. The population in far eastern DRC in 2014 was estimated to be about 5,000. However, political unrest in the DRC in recent years was accompanied by increased threats on the Grauer's and mountain gorillas from habitat loss and poaching.

    Looking at pictures of the different species of gorilla the most obvious difference between the mountain gorilla and other subspecies is the length and color of the hair. Mountain gorillas have long shaggy hair helping them deal with the cooler temperatures of the mountains compared to shorter hair in the other subspecies. Differences also include a prominent brow ridge on the mountain and western lowland gorilla and a less prominent brow ridge on the Grauer's gorilla. The Grauer's has the distinction of being the largest living primate with adult males weighing up to 500 pounds and standing up to 5' 7" tall.

A primary difference between the Bwindi gorillas of the Impenetrable Forest in Uganda and the mountain gorillas of the Virungas is their ecology and foraging behavior. In Bwindi there are more fruit bearing trees causing them to eat a greater amount of fruits and more time spent climbing. In the Virungas gorillas also climb trees to reach flowers and fruits, but not as often.

Zoologists observing mountain gorillas classify individuals into one of six age groups: infants, juveniles, adolescents, adult females, adult males (blackbacks) and silverbacks. Living mainly in family groups with an adult silverback male as the dominant leader, groups can range in size from 2 to 65 individuals. Both large and smaller groups can have more than one silverback, but only one individual is normally in charge. Some adult males become lone silverbacks.

In the Virungas 40% of the groups are multi-male and 60% are single male. Sometimes a silverback will share leadership. When leadership is shared it can be either an informal partnership or on an as need basis. For example, the Sabyinyo tourist group was led by Guhonda in 2014, the biggest silverback in the Virungas. According to my gorilla guide Olivier Nzabonimana, at one time the silverback Ryango took over leadership of the group when Guhonda was injured and unable to lead.

Adult females also have a hierarchy decided by the length of time in the group. This hierarchy can be important to the survival of the group especially when something happens to the silverback.

Adult males can weigh from 330-440 pounds (150-200 kg) and stand up to 5' 6" (1.7 m) tall. Adult females can weigh from 150-300 pounds (70-140 kg) and stand up to 5' (1.5 m) tall. Besides being almost twice the size of females, males can be distinguished from females by a large ridge of bone (sagittal crest) running lengthwise on the top of the male's head making it appear much larger.

When a male reaches about 12 years of age he begins to develop silver hair on his back, hence the name silverback. Silverbacks play a very important role in leading the group and will fight other males to retain their dominance. The silverback is supported by other males in providing support for overall group protection and in helping to herd the females to prevent them from joining other groups or lone males. At the same time the silverback is always looking for females that he can convince to come his way. The dominant silverback leads group movements and activities and

The Mountain Gorillas

helps to limit aggression between females. The average life expectancy for a male mountain gorilla is the early 30s whereas females can live into their early 40s.

Mountain gorilla social life has been well studied. When visiting with the gorillas you will be able to observe typical social behaviors such as chest beating, play, grooming and feeding. All individuals chestbeat, but it is only the silverbacks that have well-developed air sacs in their chest that reverberate the noise. One of the amusing behaviors to watch for is when a baby gorilla decides to chestbeat and then loses his or her balance in the process.

Mother gorilla and infant.

Breeding takes place year round with the female often initiating the first advance. The dominant silverback sires most offspring, although other males in the group may also father infants. Gestation lasts approximately 8.5 months. Newborn babies weigh from 3-5 pounds (1.4-2.3 kg) and are totally dependent on their mothers for the first 3 years. Generally, an infant that loses its mother during the first three years of life will not survive. Mothers will hold their newborns close to their chest and nurse them in a way similar to a human mother. Soon the baby will learn to hang on by itself climbing all over the mother including on her back. Babies will ride on their mother's back until old enough to move on their own.

After about a year babies start eating solid food. By age 2.5 to 3.5 they are completely weaned. Sadly, only about 25% of infants reach age three. Mortality results from accidents, disease and infanticide.

Infanticide occurs when a female leaves one group for another or when the silverback dies and a new silverback takes charge. The new male, who is not the father of the offspring, will usually kill it. Zoologists believe that this happens because of the silverback's desire to breed. Females with infants are not receptive to breeding. Juveniles are left unharmed since they do not influence a female's willingness to breed.

Usually a single infant is born, but twins have been recorded. A rare event took place in the Susa group on May 20, 2004 when Nyabitondore, a thirteen-year-old female, gave birth to a set of twins. When visiting the gorillas you may see babies with their mothers feeding, playing and riding on their mother's backs. Babies play with other youngsters in the group who along with older members help to teach them the ways of a gorilla. Lessons to learn include what foods to eat, how to collect those foods and how to interact with other members. Babies may also be seen playing with the silverbacks. Silverbacks show a lot of patience with the little ones and will tolerate babies climbing all over them even when they are trying to take a nap.

Presumably to help avoid inbreeding, females born in a group will often transfer to other groups. Scientific studies show that females prefer multi-male groups, a strategy that may provide increased protection to infants and more mating partners. At the same time, young females may join a lone silverback or a small group to gain status.

Adult males will often leave their group for the opportunity to start a new group or to increase their opportunities to breed. Unlike females, males cannot transfer between groups and thus must live on their own until they are able to recruit females to join them.

Baby gorillas are often seen with silverbacks.

Social interactions can have a big influence on the dynamics of a group and changes can occur quickly. For example, when I visited the Sabyinyo group in June 2005 the group had eleven members including two silverbacks, Guhonda and Ryango. Nyakalima, a lone silverback forced to leave Group 13, was trying to take females from the group. My guide told me that he was often seen nearby trying to get the attention of Kabatwa, the daughter of Guhonda. Sometimes Kabatwa would leave the group to go with Nyakalima only to return weeks later. Nyakalima died in 2008. I had hoped that someday he would lead his own group. When I visited the Sabyinyo Group in 2005 he appeared healthy even though he had a serious injury to one of his eyes from a fight with Guhonda.

I later learned that the lower ranking Sabyinyo silverback, Ryango, mysteriously left the group in April of 2006 and as of July, 2013 the group had increased in size to seventeen individuals. Ryango's disappearance was a mystery. Two subadult females, Kabatwa and Turiho, left the group for other silverbacks. Turiho went to Group 13 and Kabtwa went to a new group called Hirwa that formed in July of 2006. As of July 2013 Hirwa had sixteen members.

Gorilla Communication

When you are with the gorillas you will be able to experience many of the ways they communicate with each other. Zoologists have identified three major behaviors where communication takes place: vocalizations, facial expressions and body language. Learn the various forms of communication and listen and watch for them while you are with the group.

Many visitors miss much of what they could experience because of the time they spend taking pictures. I recommend that you absorb all that your senses will allow during the wonderful opportunity you have before you. You might even want to leave the camera behind and just focus on filling your senses. Smell the fresh mountain air, watch for how the gorillas interact with each other and savor the moment as your eyes scan the scene.

Vocalizations

While you listen for vocalizations take note of how many different sounds you can hear. A wide variety of gorilla vocalizations and sounds include close calls, barks, hoots, screams, rumbles, pig grunts, laughs and chest beats. If you want to experience these vocalizations I suggest you communicate your desire to other members in your group, including your guide. Ask them to cut down on their talking when you are with the gorillas so that you and others can better absorb the moment.

Many people overlook how important vocalizations are to understanding the social relationships in a group. DFGFI's vocalization chart that follows will also help you to have your camera ready for special behaviors like chest beating. For example, hoots are usually followed by chest beating. There are few moments when watching a group that are as special as watching a silverback run by while he beats his chest.

Hoots   Hoot series are considered a form of long distance communication. In other words, they are quite loud and often, although not exclusively, used to communicate between groups. Adult males will often hoot to announce their presence to another group. Males also use them as part of their display towards other members of their group. In both contexts, hoots generally are followed by a chest beat. Finally, hoots are also used as 'lost' calls; gorillas will hoot when they are separated from other group members.

Screams   Screams are generally used in aggressive encounters between gorillas, particularly when females or juveniles are involved. Screams are often very successful at recruiting other individuals in the group to participate in the fight. They can also scare an opponent away.

Rumble   A rumble is an example of a close call or a call that is made to communicate within the group. Rumbles are often used when gorillas find a good source of food and they will continue to make the noise throughout feeding.

Pig Grunt   This vocalization got its name because researchers thought it sounded like the grunt of a pig. Pig grunts are used to convey that an animal is mildly annoyed; for example, a pig grunt might be used to warn another individual that they have moved too close. Usually the emission of a pig grunt is enough to change the behavior of the offending individual; in this case the individual would move away. However, if the pig grunt is ignored, a louder, longer series of pig grunts may be used followed by a display or aggressive behavior.

Chest Beats Chest beats are generally seen in both adult males and juveniles. Juveniles' chest beat to other individuals as a method for soliciting play; the sound lacks the deep, resonating character you hear here because this chest beat was made by an adult male. Adult males, unlike juveniles, possess air sacks, which amplify the sound. Adult males' chest beat when displaying at group members and when communicating between groups.

Laughs Laughs are another example of a close call. Gorillas will often laugh while playing with other gorillas. This vocalization is quiet and so is often difficult to hear unless you are close to the gorillas.

The most common sound you will hear on your gorilla trek is best described as the two syllable "close call". This quiet and frequent call is given throughout the day and sounds like a human male clearing his throat. Gorilla researchers, trackers and park guides often make this sound as a calming gesture to help let the gorillas know that humans are close by and that everything is OK. Perhaps this is the best way to understand why the "close call" is so frequently heard in a group, so that members will know where everyone is and how conditions for the group at that moment are secure.

Another call given in more serious situations is described as a "bark". Barks usually are given when the gorillas feel alarmed. Barking may be used to indicate that an aggressive action may soon follow or during an actual fight. If you should hear barking sounds your guide will probably increase the number of "close call" sounds to help remind the gorillas that everything is OK, at least as far as the humans nearby are concerned.

Adult male gorillas also make a sound considered a "long call" when communicating with lone males and other groups that are within listening range. The long call is a series of powerful hoots usually accompanied by chest beating and ground thumping.

Facial Expressions

Like most primates gorillas exhibit a wide variety of facial expressions including showing teeth, opening the mouth with upper and lower teeth showing and closing the mouth with clenched teeth. Expressions of anger, happiness, aggression and anxiety can all be seen by the experienced observer. Six basic facial expressions have been described: the relaxed face, alert face, relaxed open-mouth face, pout face, staring bared-teeth scream face and compressed lip face.

Body Gestures

Gorilla body gestures include behaviors called displays that are used to communicate aggression without having to resort to violence. Displays are most frequently made by silverbacks and blackbacks and can include a number of different behaviors: hooting, strut stances, symbolic feeding, chest beating, running and tearing, and throwing vegetation while thumping on the ground.

Gorillas literally live in a salad bowl.

Gorilla Food Plants

Mountain gorillas are large-bodied herbivores. They eat an abundant supply of fresh green vegetation which results in the gorillas passing a lot of gas. Don't be surprised if you hear some funny sounding gas episodes during your visit.

Researchers have spent years studying the food habitats of the mountain gorilla. Gorillas will eat berries, various leaves, ferns and fibrous bark. Adult animals eat during a large percent of their day, making it rather easy to collect data. The hard part is identifying the plants, many species of which are still being inventoried in the park.

George Schaller and Dian Fossey were the first to identify important food plants. Continuing studies conducted by researchers at the Karisoke Research Center are helping to provide a more complete picture. One study that focused on foods eaten by gorillas near the Karisoke Center found the gorillas eating 38 species of plants from 18 families.

The Mountain Gorillas

It has been said that the gorillas literally live in a salad bowl where normally there is little problem finding something to eat. Most of the plants they eat are available year round with the notable exception of new bamboo shoots. Your park guide may point out what they are feeding on including the stems of wild celery and bamboo, the roots of nettle and the stems and roots of stinging nettle. They also eat fruits, more so at Bwindi Impenetrable National Park in Uganda, and the leaves of thistle, bamboo and Gallium vine. Food is carefully gathered using hands, lips and teeth. Many of these plants will be discussed in more detail in the chapter on plants.

In addition to eating stems, leaves and roots gorillas also feed on tree bark. I was surprised to see gorilla teeth marks on the bark of the eucalyptus trees that were growing along the edge of the park. This same tree species grows in my front yard in Texas. Now every time I look at my tree I am reminded not only of the koalas that eat the eucalyptus trees in Australia, but also of the gorillas in Rwanda.

Mountain gorillas have been observed eating non-plant items including driver ants, the cocoons of unknown invertebrates and fine subsoil sediments that may provide a source of sodium and iron.

The following species are some of the most important staple food plants for the park's gorillas:

Celery, *Peucedanum linderi* (stems and roots)
Carduus nyassanus var ruandensis (leaves, stems and roots)
Galium chloroianthum
Galium simense
Galium spurium L. subsp africanum (all parts)
Woodnettle, *Laportea alatipes* (leaves)
Rubus kirungensis (leaves, stems and fruits)
Rubus runssorensis var. umbrosus (leaves, stems and fruits)
Bamboo, *Yushania alpina* (shoots)
Carex bequaertii (leaves, flowers and stems)
Lobelia giberroa HEMSLEY (pith)

Juvenile gorilla feeding on vine.

>*Dendrosenecio adnoivaris* (Pith)
>*Rumex bequartii* (stems)
>*Vernonia adolfi-frederici* (pith, flowers)
>*Crassocephalum dulcis-aprutii* (stems)
>*Discopodium penninervum* (pith)
>*Helicrisum sp* (leaves and stems)
>*Hypericum revolutum* (bark)

THE MOUNTAIN GORILLAS

A day in the life of a Gorilla

A day in the life of a gorilla is divided up into periods of feeding, resting and traveling. Feeding is a prime activity when the family wakes up at sunrise. The earlier your gorilla trek begins the greater your chance will be in seeing feeding behavior. No matter when you arrive, even if it is during a rest period you will see plenty of activity. Often times while the silverback and other adults are trying to rest the infants and juveniles can be observed in various forms of play. Fun and learning experience activities can include climbing all over the body of a sleeping silverback, swinging from vines, climbing on small trees, tumbling and learning how to run and chest beat at the same time. Rest periods are important to the cohesiveness of the group as they help to reinforce social bonds while allowing for play and mutual grooming.

Juvenile gorilla resting at mid day.

As you approach the gorillas, watch for trampled down areas where they have been feeding. The vegetation may look well worked over, but never to the point where all of the plants have been completely removed. Re-growth rates are augmented by high rainfall allowing flattened areas to quickly grow back.

The day ends for the gorillas with groups making nests and settling down for the night about an hour before sunset. Very few park visitors have seen this activity since nearly all gorilla treks return by mid-afternoon or earlier. Watch for nests as you approach your group. You might be fortunate to see a fresh nest from the night before.

Home Ranges

Group home ranges average about 3 square miles (8 km²) depending on the quality of the habitat. The gorillas are always on the move in finding new feeding areas. Daily movements can vary from .12 - 1.24 miles (200 to 2000 meters). Normally groups will stay in a small area 1-2 days and return months later allowing the vegetation to recover.

Gorillas in the Virungas travel less than gorillas at Bwindi Impenetrable National Park where home ranges are up to 15.5 square miles (40 km²) per year. Group ranges often overlap resulting in group interactions where travel routes intersect. These interactions are not considered territorial in nature, just chance encounters. Such interactions are often aggressive, with males making displays and vocalizing as they try to protect their group while encouraging prospective females to transfer over. Females often will transfer without any encouragement and will do so when they are ready to leave. Changes within a group from these interactions and other events occur often enough to keep gorilla researchers and park guides on their toes. As a result, interaction events combined with deaths from old age, disease, infanticide and poaching can make life for a researcher very challenging. In one message from a friend with whom I exchange e-mails and who works in the park, he wrote "Sorry I haven't been in touch, but the last three months of 2006 were horrible with gorillas separating, joining new groups, many deaths."

DFGFI periodically reports on group interactions in website Field Reports and other communications to its members. When I visited the Susa Group in 2003 I just missed the chance of seeing a dramatic meeting between the Susa and the Pablo Groups, the

The Mountain Gorillas

two largest groups in the Virungas. At the time Susa had 35 individuals and Pablo had 57. I can just imagine the excitement of seeing over 90 mountain gorillas in one area, what a photo opportunity that would have made, especially if they were in an open area where all the group members could see each other! On August 28, 2004 DFGFI reported another interaction between the Susa and Pablo Groups. According to the report there were many interactions between the males, but "none of the males who participated sustained any wounds, and no females changed groups".

Individual gorillas are identified through nose prints which are as varied and unique as finger prints in humans.

Gorilla Groups

During a six-week period in March and April of 2010 a new gorilla census in the Virunga Volcanoes range spanning the borders of Rwanda, Uganda and the Eastern Democratic Republic of Congo estimated a mountain gorilla population of 480 individuals. At that time there were sixteen habituated groups (269 individuals), twelve unhabituated groups (80 individuals) and eleven lone silverbacks. That census revealed a 26.3 % increase in the seven years since the last count in 2003.

Mountain gorilla groups in Volcanoes National Park are monitored by RDB, DFGFI and the International Gorilla Conservation Program (IGCP). Rwandan military provides security for tourists on treks to see the habituated gorillas. Each gorilla known to park staff and researchers studying the gorillas - mainly the habituated groups - is monitored and studied.

Naming

To help monitor their movements, each gorilla is given a name. Individual gorillas are identified through nose prints which are as varied and unique as finger prints in humans. Until recently, naming baby gorillas was the sole responsibility of park staff, but in 2005 RDB initiated an annual gorilla naming ceremony giving individuals and corporations naming rights as part of a new fund raising effort to help promote conservation and tourism.

In addition to funds generated by tourists staying in hotels and lodges, Rwandans living near the park benefit from park permit revenues (5% from every permit). These funds are used to support socio-economic projects in surrounding communities such as projects to benefit schools and water supplies. RDB reported in 2013 that tourism in Rwanda is the highest source of foreign currency in the country. In 2012, over 22,000 tourists came to Rwanda mainly to see the mountain gorillas. Tourism in Rwanda grew by 17% over 2011 helping to provide significant support for conservation efforts throughout the country.

On June 25th 2005, RDB held its first Gorilla Naming and Fundraising Ceremony. The fundraising effort was a great success and raised over $1.4 Million (US). Twenty-eight new baby gorillas were named and funds were designated for priority projects. New gorilla names are first proposed by the group's trackers. Each name reflects a moment in recent history or something special about the conditions of the birth or the group's dynamics. The DFGFI Field Notes that follow help to shed some light on how the new names are chosen. Most of the names below were picked by DFGFI staff before the naming ceremony was initiated in 2005.

Turibamwe: Maggie's infant, who was born into Pablo's group in 2005. The name means "we are all the same" in Kinyarwanda and represents the spirit of unity in the country after its difficult recent history.

Afrika (Africa): born 20th April 2000. This baby was born during a time whenUganda and Rwanda were fighting in DRC. This baby was named in recognition of the sadness the staff felt about this conflict.

Imvune (infiltrations): born 15th August 1999. Refers to the hard conditions the KRC trackers and other residents of Musanze endured during 1997 and 1998.

Irakoze (thanks to God): born 4th May 2000. Named for the release of a Karisoke employee from prison, and how all the staff welcomed his return to his family, hisfriends and Karisoke.

Isaro (pearl): born 17th May 1999. Strong and beautiful. The Volcanoes NationalPark is the pearl of Rwanda and is a major source of income through tourism.

Kumenya (to know): born 27th January 1999. In recognition of the trackers beingable to identify the gorillas after a long period away from their work in the park.

Mafunzo (training): born 18th June 1999. KRC trackers were undergoing paramilitary training when this infant was born to Puck.

Pato (to wait): born 18th January 2000. Shangaza was 19 years old, 10 years older before giving birth to this, her first surviving infant.

Ruhuka (holiday): born 15th October 1999, because the Karisoke director was onleave when she was born.

Taraja (hope & expectation): born 1st June 1999. Hope and expectation is for the future of KRC, its trackers, their lives and the survival of the mountain gorillas.

Tegereza (end of the century): born 25th October 1999. Y2K! This name was chosen because some say we are nearing the end of the world and others say it isn't. So the KRC trackers were waiting to see what happened at the end of 1999.

Umutekano (security): born 13th November 1999. To mark the restoration of peace in northwestern Rwanda after the insecurity of 1997-98.

Umwe (in memory of Dian Fossey): born 13th March 2000. Named in remembrance of Dian Fossey, the work she did and how at this time the gorilla population seems to be slowly increasing.

During the summer of 2014, RDB hosted the Tenth Annual Gorilla Naming Ceremony when Rwanda celebrated not only many new baby gorillas, but also the 26.3% growth in the gorilla population since 2003. The event also recognized and rewarded international tourists and conservation organizations who have visited the country and the great role they have played in conserving the gorillas through tourism.

Gorilla Groups Habituated for Tourism

When I first visited the gorillas in 1989 our guide spoke mainly French. It was not until Bill and Amy Vedder published their book *In the Kingdom of Gorillas* that I was able to learn more about Group 11, the first group I saw in 1989. In putting this book together I realized that there was little information available on the makeup and history of the groups habituated for tourism in Rwanda. As of June 1, 2014 RDB listed ten gorilla families available for tourists including two of the nine research groups. They included the nine member Bwenge Group, led by the silverback Bwenge who was a son of the famous silverback Titus, and the Ugenda Group with eight.

Group 11 (1978-1996)

Group 11 was named by a gorilla survey team conducting a census on Mt. Visoke in 1978. There were 12 gorillas in the group. In 1979 when RDB decided to habituate gorillas for tourism, Group 11 was one of the first groups tourists were able to visit. The silverback in this group was named Stilgar for the powerful yet serene ruler from the novel *Dune*. Gorilla researcher Craig Sholley gave Stilgar his English name with the rest of the family members receiving African names. Each name reflected group status, physical characteristics, or individual personalities: a second silverback named Ndume – meaning male for the next in line; Kosa for her missing hand; Kadele for her constant vocalizations; Sababu, Kadele's baby and "the reason" for her vocalizations; Furaha or "joy"; Nshuti for best friend of Furaha; and Tano for being fifth in line.

By the time I returned to Rwanda in 2003 Group 11 was no longer listed as a tourist group. According to an RDB tracker and guide who has worked in the park for nearly ten years, many believe that Group 11 moved to the Congo in 1996 and has not been documented on the Rwanda side since.

Amahoro Group

In 1996 a team of trackers began the process of habituating a 16-member group of gorillas living along the slopes of Mt. Bisoke. In 2002 the group split into two when Amahoro, the dominant silverback, died and two subordinate silverbacks each took part of the group. The silverback Ubumwe ended up taking over the group with the second silverback Charles taking two females to form his own group. During this period there were peaceful interactions between the two groups which continue today.

On June 25, 2005 at the first formal RDB naming ceremony the group led by Charles was named Umubano, meaning relationship. After Charles formed his new group he began looking for new females and gained one female from an unhabituated group. He also interacted with the Shinda Research Group where he lost two females. In July, 2013 the Amahoro Group had 19 members.

Agashya Group (formerly Group 13)

Agashya Group has 23-members and lives on the slopes of Mt. Sabyinyo and Mt. Gahinga. The silverback Munani died in 2003 and for a short time was led by blackback Nyakarima. A little over three months later a lone silverback named Agashya took over. Up until he died in 2008 Nyakarima was a lone silverback following both the Sabyinyo Group and Agasha Group. Visitors to the Sabyinyo and Agasha often saw him nearby. When Munani was alive the group was called Group 13.

After Agashya took over Group 13 he brought to the group two females with one baby. Two babies in this group were born in 2005. An offspring of Rugendo was born on December 21, 2005. The offspring of Safari was born on March 11, 2005. Safari was named by Dian Fossey in 1979.

In approaching this group trekkers normally pass through a large bamboo forest.

Sabyinyo Group

The Sabyinyo Group is led by Guhonda who is believed by many to be the largest silverback in Volcanoes National Park and weighs over 400 pounds (181 kg). According to RDB records on February 1, 2014 Guhonda will be 43 years old. There are sixteen members in the group and they oftentimes can be found in the lower elevations of the bamboo forest. On July 1, 2013 a new baby was born to the 12 year-old female Kampanga.

Nyakarima, a lone silverback who was forced to leave Group 13 in 2003, was trying to take females from the Sabyinyo Group and Group 13. He was often seen near both groups. The Sabyinyo Group was featured in the *Saving a Species: Gorillas on the Brink* Animal Planet documentary with animal expert Jack Hanna and actress Natalie Portman and in a Discovery Channel documentary in 2005 with Sigourney Weaver.

During the time that I visited Rwanda in 2003 and 2005 I spent most of my time visiting the Sabyinyo Group while working on this book. You can watch a 2003 trek I filmed visiting the group in a three part video at www.youtube.com/ricklobello.

Susa and Karisimbi Groups

The Susa Group was first discovered along the Susa River and was featured in the film *Gorillas in the Mist*. Originally studied by Fossey, in 2014 it was the largest tourist group in the park with 37 members and the only surviving twin mountain gorillas. Kurira was the dominant silverback and the subdominant silverback was Igisha. All together there were three silverbacks in the group. In late 2009 the group split into two groups with Susa Group A having 27 members and Group B having 14. Group B is now called the Karisimbi Group. On April 18, 2012 Karisimbi split into two groups. As of July 2013 the Susa Group had 37 members, Karismibi had 12 and the new group called the Isimbi Group had 8 members. Like with all the gorilla groups they are normally easier to find during the months of March-May and September-December when bamboo shoots are available in the lower elevations of the park.

Because of the size of the group there were many females with babies allowing for greater possibilities of viewing mother and baby interactions and babies at play. A rare event took place in this group on May 20, 2004 when Nyabitondore, a thirteen-year-old female, gave birth to a set of twins. The survival chances for gorilla twins are very limited, but these twins were doing well and were named by President Paul Kagame and his wife at the first international gorilla naming ceremony in 2005: Byishimo meaning happiness and Impano meaning gift.

At that time the 41 member group interacted with the Pablo Group, a research group with 42 members and not available for tourists. When this happened there were up to 83 gorillas in the same area. In 2014 the Susa Group and the Pablo Group were still the two largest groups in the Virungas.

This area of the Virungas has the highest rate of gorilla reproduction in the park. Nyabitondore, a twenty-three-year-old female, is the daughter of Picasso, a gorilla that was studied by Dian Fossey. In early 2009 she transferred to the Pablo Group. Another, 7-year-old female, Isonga, is the daughter of Poppy, also studied by Dian Fossey. At the time they were studied by Fossey both Picasso and Poppy were members of Group Five.

Gorilla group sizes and some members may change every year. When you arrive at park headquarters ask at the reception desk for the latest information on the number of gorillas in each group. You may be able to request seeing a particular group.

Umbano Group

Umubano is led by a silverback named Charles. The group was formed in 2002 when the Amahoro Group split in two after the death of Amahoro. At that time Charles was one of two subordinate silverbacks. Charles took two females with him to form his own group leaving the second dominant silverback Ubumwe with the rest. Since the formation of the two groups there have been peaceful interactions between the groups and those interactions continue today. Charles was named for a tracker who helped to habituate this 12-member group.

After Charles formed his new group he began looking for new females. He interacted with an unhabituated group gaining one female. He also interacted with the Shinda Research Group when he lost two females. Later these females came back to him.

A new baby was born to this group on June 4, 2011.

Hirwa Group

This group of 16 gorillas formed in June 2006. A silverback named Munyinya that left the Susa Group and then took females from the Sabyinyo and Agashya groups, started the group which now has eight females, three juveniles and four babies. A new baby was born on February 7, 2012.

Kwitonda Group

The 23-member Kwitonda Group crossed over from the DRC in 2005. Two babies were born in the group the following year in May and November. Kwitonda means "humble one" and in 2013 the group had three silverbacks, one blackback, seven adult females, two subadult females, three juveniles and seven babies. It is a peaceful group that is expected to grow in size.

Research Groups

Few people other than gorilla researchers and park staff have had the opportunity to see the gorilla research groups monitored and studied by DFGFI in cooperation with RDB. The continuing long term monitoring of these groups is critical to the success of mountain gorilla conservation in the Virungas. Having research groups that are not visited by tourists ensures the continued and uninterrupted data collection that began in 1967 with Dian Fossey. It also helps to ensure that a subset of the population is not exposed on a daily basis to international travelers who may carry illnesses. Research on these groups represents the world's most intense long-term study of any large animal. Descriptions of these groups are included in the previous chapter on Dian Fossey. For the latest information on how they are doing follow the DFGF Blog link from the Site Map at www.gorillafund.org .

On April 20, 2008 the incredible life story of Titus of Beetsme's Group premiered on TV in the NATURE series, *The Gorilla King,* a documentary narrated by Academy Award-winning actor F. Murray Abraham. No other nature documentary ever made can claim to retrace the life of a mountain gorilla over a 33 year period. If you missed seeing it you can buy your own copy on High Definition DVD. Up until he died Titus held the fatherhood record of all time having sired more babies than any mountain gorilla on record.

The Fate of Fossey's Other Gorillas

In her book *Gorillas in the Mist* Dian Fossey describes her observations of numerous gorillas that she knew and studied from 1967 to 1981. The following information summarizes what has happened to selected individuals since the book's publication in 1982.

Augustus
Transfer to UNKNOWN (UNKNOWN location) – August 16, 1985. She left Group 4 in 1978.

Beethoven
Died sometime in August 1985 of old age.

Effie
Died sometime in April 1994 of old age. Lived in Group Five until it split in May 1993; then lived in Pablo's group until death. She had many offspring including a Female (MAH) born October 20, 1984 and Female (TUY) born March 21, 1989.

Peanuts group feeding in the giant senecio zone above 11,000 feet on Mt Visoke.

Flossie
Died December 1, 1989 of old age. Transfer to GROUP 5 on Nov. 5, 1985. Offspring – Female (UMW) born June 1, 1983; Male (VAT) born October 19, 1986; Infant (I10) born September 25, 1988; Premature.

Fuddle
Died October 23, 2002 of old age. Transfer to TIGER'S GROUP on June 15, 1985. Transfer to BEETSME'S GROUP on April 15, 1987. Offspring – Male (NBA) born February 15, 1986; Male (JOA) born February 23, 1988; Male (RAN) born August 10, 1992; Female (TAR) born June 1, 1999.

Icarus
Died sometime in November 1983 due to unknown causes.

Nunkie
Died May 27, 1985 of unknown causes.

Pantsy
Died sometime in February 1999 of old age. Lived in group 5 until split in May 1993; then lived in Pablo's group. Offspring – Male (UMR) born January 4, 1986. Female (NOE) born December 7, 1989; Male (TUR) born March 18, 1991. Male (GIC) born May 11, 1995.

Pablo
Last seen on July 13, 2008 when he left the group with another silverback. DFGFI announced that he was presumed dead in their fall 2008 newsletter.

Peanuts
Died on May 1, 1989 of old age.

Puck
Died of cancer on April 10, 2007. Lived in Group 5 until split in May 1993; then lived in Pablo's group. Offspring – Female (INT) born February 12, 1986; Female (MAK) born August 20, 1989; Male (ISA) born October 12, 1992; Male (GSG) born June 27, 1996; Male (MAF) born June 18, 1999; Female (NDW) born February 25, 2003.

Shinda
Died of natural causes on November 24, 2008.

Simba
Died on November 17, 1999 of unknown causes. Transferred to TIGER'S group on August 3, 1984. Transferred to GROUP 5 on December 21, 1984. When Group 5 split in 1993, went to Shinda's group. Offspring – Female (IMA) born May 31, 1986; Male (INS)

born February 4, 1988; Male (TWI) born May 7, 1992; Three infants born between INS and TWI that didn't survive.

Tuck

Died September 5, 2010, one of Fossey's original research subjects. Offspring–Male born February 16, 1985; Unknown sex (I09) born July 24, 1988; Premature; Female (UMC) born August 24, 1989; Male (TUT) born August 20, 1992; Stillborn; Male (VUB) born August 28, 1993; Male (DSR) born July 25, 1997; Male (URS) born April 5, 2001; Male (SEG) born October 8, 2005.

Ziz

Died on May 21, 1993. Following his death Group 5 split and became Pablo's and Shinda's groups.

Ziz, Silverback 'stands guard' as his family group moves through open areas of the forest - from one feeding area to another.

Dense vegetation in the Virungas.

    Rwanda is a very green country. Everywhere you look you can see rich agricultural lands with dark soil and tall trees along the roadsides. The impact of humans on the landscape can be seen everywhere. Go to Google Earth and scan for the big picture where satellite images show the park as a green island surrounding by a sea of agriculture, a dramatic backdrop to the country's protected areas and parks.

    Few people visiting Volcanoes National Park spend time learning about the plants. Park guides are limited in their knowledge of botany and are familiar mainly with the primary gorilla food plants and some of the more common trees. They'll point out nettles, bamboo and Hagenia trees, but little else. That's why this part of the book is so important. Understanding the flora that holds this ecosystem together is critical to understanding and conserving the park.

Hypericum lancelatum trees with a species of Lobelia in the foreground on the slopes of Mount Karisimbi.

Plants of Volcanoes National Park

Rwanda's Volcanoes National Park helps to protect about 62 square miles (160 km²) or 36% of the 170 square mile (440 km²) forested area that makes up the Virunga ecosystem. The combined area mountain gorillas inhabit totals about 145 square miles (375 km²). That's not a very large area. For comparison sake, New York City is twice the size of the habitat occupied by the mountain gorillas.

Researchers who have compiled plant and animal data on what is currently known about the biodiversity of the park describe the Virungas as one of the most diverse habitats in the world. The transboundary park area is best understood as one ecosystem. A biological survey undertaken early in 2004 includes detailed inventories of the animals and plants. It was compiled as a cooperative effort by the Wildlife Conservation Society (WCS), Dian Fossey Gorilla Fund International (DFGFI), Institut Congolais pour la Conservation (ICCN), The Rwanda Development Board (RDB), Uganda Wildlife Authority (UWA), Institute of Tropical Forest Conservation (ITFC) and the International Gorilla Conservation Program (IGCP). Every year that research continues helps the park gain additional information important to its long term protection.

Biologists describe habitats using the dominant vegetation patterns that they find from one area to the next. Plant diversity is determined by the quality and makeup of the soil, sun exposure, geology, elevation and climate. The Virungas have been carefully studied over the years and eight different plant communities have been described. At least one hundred and twenty-four species are endemic including some that are threatened.

Of these eight communities, five vegetation zones have been described in the mountainous areas of Volcanoes National Park. Depending on how close your gorilla group is to the park's boundary, you may have to walk up through three different vegetation zones: the lower Mixed Forest, Bamboo and Hagenia-Hypericum Zones. The gorillas prefer the lower elevations and rarely go above 10,991 ft (3,350 m).

Mixed Forest Zone (Ficalhoa Forest)

The lowest elevation zone from 5,249 to 9,186 ft (1600-2800m) is called the Mixed Forest Zone. This moist zone is dominated by semi-deciduous broad-leaf trees and a wide variety of herbaceous plants. Most of the plants and animals in this zone have been eliminated by people who have cleared the land for agriculture. At Volcanoes National Park, a relic band of mixed forest is dominated by broad-leafed semi-deciduous trees found mainly in a small area between Mts. Gahinga and Sabyinyo. This zone is also known as the Afro-montane forest. Typical trees of this zone include *Ficalhoa laurifolia* and *Afrocrania volkensii*. Larger expanses of this important zone are still intact in the DRC and in Uganda at Bwindi Impenetrable National Park.

Baby gorilla climbing a bamboo stalk.

Bamboo Zone

From 8,202 to 9,186 ft (2500-2800m) the Bamboo Zone is covered with mono-specific stands of bamboo and grassy meadows. There are 1,600 known species of bamboo around the world. With so many people familiar with bamboo this zone is the easiest of the five zones to identify. The zone is approximately .3 miles (.5 km) wide with little undergrowth. Bamboo (*Yushania alpina*) stands are favorite feeding areas for the gorillas when fresh shoots appear during the rainy seasons of March-May and September-December.

PLANTS OF VOLCANOES NATIONAL PARK

Hagenia-Hypericum Zone

Higher up, at 9,186 to 10,499 ft (2800-3200m), the Hagenia-Hypericum Zone is dominated by open canopy woodland with large Hagenia (*Hagenia abyssinica*) and *Hypericum revolutum* trees. Intermixed in this woodland are numerous species of herbaceous plants and grasses, many of which are rich in gorilla foods. The Karisoke Research Camp that Dian Fossey established in 1967 is located in this zone.

Subalpine Zone

The two highest zones are the Subalpine Zone at 10,499 to 11,811 ft (3200-3600m) and the Alpine Zone above 11,811 ft (3600m). The Subalpine Zone has an abundance of

Bamboo forest in the lower elevations of the park.

small tree-sized plants with broad leaves and tall trunks. To many, the plants in this zone resemble some of the succulents found in the desert Southwest of the United States. The dominant species include: *Senecio johnstonii, Lobelia stuhlmanni, Lobelia wollostonii, Rubus kirungensis* and *Hypericum revolutum*. Very few park visitors see this zone since it rarely is used by the mountain gorillas. As habitat is reduced in lower elevations use of this zone may increase. This is not good for the gorillas because of the cold and bad for the plants, many of which have taken hundreds of years to reach their current size.

Alpine Zone

The Alpine Zone above 11,811' (3600m) is covered by low grasses and mosses, an occasional *Senecio johnstonii* and bare rocky areas. Mountain gorillas use all vegetation zones except the Alpine Zone and only those people who have the time and the energy to climb the volcanoes have been to the top of the Virungas.

Common Plants of Volcanoes National Park

The plant list included online at www.iloveparks.com/rwanda includes species of plants botanists have thus far identified in the park. Plant species that are eaten by the gorillas are shown in bold. The easiest plants in the park to identify are the Hagenia trees, giant lobelia, bamboo, ferns, Gallium vines and nettles. The park's plant list will no doubt grow over time as researchers continue their work inventorying and identifying what they find. For the entire Albertine Rift region, over 5,800 plant species have been identified.

Protecting rainforest habitat is important to people as a source of current and future compounds used by physicians looking for new ways to prevent and cure human ailments and diseases. Seventy percent of the plants identified by the U.S. National Cancer Institute as useful in the treatment of cancer are found only in rainforests. Could it be possible that someday we may learn from gorilla eating habits that some of the medicinal plants they eat are also important to people? One of the interesting topics park researchers are studying is how animals will seek plants that have medicinal properties. For all five subspecies of gorillas researchers have identified 118 species of food plants with medicinal values. At Volcanoes National Park 31 of the 113 known species of medicinal plants are eaten by the mountain gorillas and some movements of gorillas to different parts of their habitat may be motivated by these plants.

Volcanoes National Park Gorilla Food Plants with Medicinal Values

Basella alba
Carduus leptocanthus
Carica cundinamarcensis Linden ex Hook. F
Clematis hirsuta Perr et Guill
Clematis simensis
Clerodendron johnstonii
Crassocephalum manii
Discopodium penninervium
Dombea goetzenii
Dracaena afromontana
Gynura scandens
Hagenia abyssinica
Hypericum peplidifolium
Hypericum revolutum
Impatiens burtonii
Lobelia giberroa
Maesa lanceolata
Momordica pterocarpa
Oreosyce Africana
Plantago palmate
Plectranthus laxiflorus
Polygonum nepalense
Rubus kirungensis
Solanum anguivii
Solanum nigrum

Urera hypselodendron
Urtica massaica
Vernonia adolfi-frederici
Vernonia auriculifera
Yushania alpina Schumann
Zehneria scabra

Popular field guides designed to help the layperson identify the plants of this region of Africa are not available at this time. If you see a plant and want to learn more about it your best chance of getting some help would be to send a photograph of the plant to the Karisoke Research Center in Rwanda by first contacting DFGFI.

Selected Common Plants of Volcanoes National Park

For a complete list of plants visit www.iloveparks.com/rwanda.

Trees and other large Plants

Eucalyptus, *Syzygium parviflorum*
Local Name: Inturusu
Description: A tall evergreen tree with grayish waxy leaves. Leaves form in pairs on opposite sides of a square stem. Brown colored bark grows in layers.
Special Notes: This very common and tall tree is found throughout Rwanda mainly along roadsides and at shambas (farms). Along with other exotic trees like cypress and pine, about 0.6 % of the park area is covered with non-native plants. Eucalyptus is native to Australia, New Guinea, Indonesia and the Philippine Islands where there are over 700 species. It grows very quickly and is often used as an ornamental or as a windbreak. It is well known as a food plant for Australia's popular little marsupial, the koala. In the park area it grows along the boundary where gorillas will sometimes feed on its bark. Eucalyptus trees surround the Gorillas Nest lodge near park headquarters at Kinigi.

Cypress tree, *Cinara cupressi*
Description: A tall evergreen tree with orange to reddish brown bark and needle-like leaves typical of conifers.
Special Notes: Like with the eucalyptus tree, several exotic cypress tree species have been widely planted in Rwanda as windbreaks in areas where there have been attempts to reforest the country with fast growing trees.

Silverback feeding on a eucalyptus tree.

Hagenia tree, *Hagenia abyssinica*

Local Names: Umugeshi, in English as African redwood, brayera, cusso, hagenia, or kousso.

Description: Hagnenias are slender trees with umbrella shaped crowns that can grow up to 66 feet (20 m). They have compound leaves up to 15.75 inches (40 cm) long with 7-13 long serrated 4 inch (10 cm) leaflets. Flowers are white to orange growing in 11.8-23.6 inch (30-60 cm) panicles. These twisted gnarled trees that George Schaller said give "the appearance of a kindly unkempt man," are often densely covered with mosses, lichens and epiphytes.

Rare mature Hagenia trees at Karisoke. This is the same place where Bob Campbell took the National Geographic cover (1970) photo of Dian Fossey with Coco and Pucker.

Special Notes: This tree is found at 9,186 to 10,499 ft (2800-3200m) where in many areas like the saddle area around the Karisoke Research Camp it is the most common tree. Hagenia trees are commonly seen in photographs of Karisoke and other dramatic vista areas of the Virungas. The most conspicuous tree in the Virungas, gorillas will climb Hagenias and feed on both flowers and leaves. These trees also provide habitat niches for other plants including orchids, ferns, mosses, lichen and animals like hyrax, mongoose and squirrels. Gorillas will use the hollowed openings at the base of large tree trunks for shelter. Hagenia is a well-known treatment in East Africa for tapeworms in humans and livestock.

Guide to Rwanda's Volcanoes National Park

St. John's Wort, Rose of Sharon and Tutsan, *Hypericum revolutum*

Local Name: Umushunguru

Description: This is a smaller and much more delicate tree compared to the Hagenia. Trees reach up to 39 feet (12 m) and have pointed, opposite and simple oval leaves that are often densely laden with *Usnea* sp. lichens.

Special Notes: This plant is used exclusively as a food supply for several moth species. The bark of the tree is a staple for the gorillas. The flowers are available year round and are eaten by mountain gorillas and golden monkeys. The tree is often host to *Englerina woodfordioides*, a parasitic species of mistletoe with red flowers and fruits and an important food for the gorillas.

Giant Hagenia tree branch covered in epiphytes including moss, Usnea lichen, hanging ferns (Polypodium, eaten by gorillas) and pink orchids.

PLANTS OF VOLCANOES NATIONAL PARK

Vernonia adolfi-frederic
Local Name: Igiheriheri
Description: Trees have rather rough and longitudinally flaking light gray bark and may reach 25-30 feet (7.6-9.1 m). Leaves are oblong and flowers are creamy white and thistlelike.
Special Notes: The pith and flowers of this tree are a staple food for the gorillas. *Vernonia* trees are the third most common tree on the slopes of Visoke near the saddle at Karisoke. Fossey reported how gorillas favored the flower buds and plucked them off one by one like humans eating grapes. Gorillas also eat the pulp and decaying wood of dead trees. Fossey found many clumps of broken *Vernonia* stumps indicating former areas where gorillas once concentrated.

Ficalhoa laurifolia
Local Name: Umuhumba
Description: Small tree with reddish brown bark and longitudinal fissures. Glossy leaves are lancelate to ovate.
Special Notes: This species is closely related to *Camellia sinensis* whose leaves are used to produce a tea. Trees are exploited for housing, furniture and beehive making materials.

Giant Senecio, *Senecio mariettae, Senecio subsessilis*
Local Names: Umubatura (*mariettae*), Igihuna, Igitamatama
Description: This yucca-like tree grows up to 12 feet (3.5 m) tall. Like yucca and palm trees, the dead leaves collapse along the trunk. Special Notes: Gorillas will periodically range to the higher Subalpine Zone just to eat the pith of the senecios. Plants in this genus contain alkaloids which have stimulating effects upon the entire body. There is very little else for the gorillas to eat in this zone and as a result they may seek the plant for its stimulating effects.

Green mountain bamboo, *Yushania alpina*
Local Name: Umugano
Description: An evergreen clump forming bamboo growing up to 33 feet (10 m) tall.
Special Notes: Gorillas eat the tender shoots of bamboo during the rainy seasons of

Green mountain bamboo.

March-May and September-December. Bamboo is one of the most important food plants for the gorillas during these periods when the plant may account for up to 90 per cent of their diet. Bamboo is also a valuable material to people who use it for building houses and making baskets and mats. Some people living nearby will illegally cut bamboo in the park. Illegal activities like collecting bamboo threaten the gorillas' food supply. The plant is also used to make illegal snares which can seriously injure the gorillas. Bamboo is found mainly along the eastern park boundary and is responsible for the seasonal movements of many of the habituated tourist and research gorilla groups.

Giant lobelias growing along the crater rim on the top of Mount Mgahinga.

Banana, *Ensete ventricosum*
Local Name: Igitembe
Description: Plants with very large leaves grow up to 26 feet (8 m) tall.
Special Notes: Bananas are grown in Rwanda, but are not a native food for the gorillas. Banana beer is popular in many parts of the country.

Giant lobelia, *Lobelia giberroa*
Description: Lobelia can easily grow over 10 feet (3.5 m) tall. The plant has dense multiple flower covered stalks growing out of a rosette of long pointed leaves that grow attached to the trunk.

Special Notes: These beautiful succulents look like a cross between a yucca plant with its large leaves and a sotol plant with its tall flower stalk, two widespread plants of the Southwest United States. Gorillas feed on four of the seven species of *Lobelia* in the park. *Lobelia giberroa*, growing in the lower elevations, is a staple food for the gorillas. They eat the plant by snapping off the tall flower stalk and eating the soft pith at the base of the leaves. They will also pull up the root and peel off the bark.

Smaller Plants

Thistle, *Carduus nyassanus var ruandensis*
Local Names: Ikigwarara, Mugabudasumirwa
Description: Thistles are weedy plants with prickly-winged stems and leaves and variously colored flower heads surrounded by prickly bracts.
Special Notes: Thistles in the park look like familiar thistles growing in other parts of the world. Gorillas eat the entire plant and have little problem dealing with the spiny stems and leaves. They also eat the roots. The flowers attract butterflies and the larvae that hatch later are a favorite food of the mountain gorilla.

Sourdock, Common Sorrel, *Rumex abyssinicus, Rumex abyssinicus, Rumex usambarensis, Rumex ruwenzoriensis*
Local Names: Umufumba, Nyiramuko
Description: These erect plants have long tap roots and fleshy to leathery leaves. Flowers are tiny and inconspicuous and grow in whorl-like clusters.
Special Notes: Four species of Rumex are found in the park: *Rumex abyssinicus, Rumex abyssinicus, Rumex usambarensis, Rumex ruwenzoriensis*. Gorillas feed on the stems of all but *ruwenzoriensis*.

Gorillas feed on four different species of thistle (Carduus) in the Virungas.

Stinging nettles, *Boehmeria macrophylla, Droguetia iners, Girardinia bullosa, Laportea alatipes, Pilea rivularis, Urera cameroonensis, Urera hypselodendron, Urtica massaica* (All identified as foods for gorillas)

Local Names: Umuse, Mayonza, Igisura, Ikibabanzomvu, Umurishafumberi

Description: These stout plants seem to grow almost everywhere. They are 2-4 feet (.61-1.22 m) tall with heart-shaped, long-stalked and dark green papery leaves with coarse teeth and stinging hairs on both the stems and leaves.

Special Notes: Gorillas are known to eat eight of the eighteen species of nettles in the park. Unlike people who wear gloves and thick clothing to protect their skin, gorillas amazingly have little problem dealing with the tiny, nearly invisible stinging hairs.

Wild celery, *Peucedanum linderi*
Local Name: Igisengosengo
Description: Wild celery bares little resemblance to the celery people buy at the grocery store. The plants are long, limp and flat and have a green mid-ridge.
Special Notes: Gorillas eat the stems and roots of two of the four species of wild celery in the park.

Pyrethrum, *Chrysanthemum coccineum*
Description: Plants have blue-green leaves and grow up to 17 – 24 inches (45-60 cm) in height. The flowers look like white daisies.
Special Notes: This plant was brought into the country by Europeans in the 1940s and is one of the safest insecticides for use around food. Unfortunately for the park, much of the area was converted to pyrethrum during the last century resulting in the loss of habitat important to gorillas and other creatures. Fossey reported that 22,000 acres were removed from the park in 1969 to make room for larger plantations. Most of this area was probably covered with important areas of bamboo.

Galium, *Galium chloroianthum*, *Galium simense*, Galium spurium L. subsp africanum
Local Name: Urukararambwe
Description: Large oval leafed plant growing in vines. Special Notes: There are seven species of *Galium* in the park, three of which are known to be eaten by the gorillas. *Galium* is a staple food for the gorillas and is easily identified by park visitors who often see the gorillas pull on the plant's vines as they eat the stems and the leaves.

BIRDS OF VOLCANOES NATIONAL PARK

My favorite bird in Rwanda is the Crowned Crane. I saw my first one alongside a stream on the road between Kigali and Musanze. With its round white cheek patches, black cap, red throat and fancy head dress, it's one of the most beautiful cranes in the world. When I stayed at the Gorilla's Nest Lodge several Crowned Cranes kept me company during a quiet travel week in February. They were joined by a dozen or so Pied Crows and a white domestic cat that was playing a "dare you get too close" game with the crows on the roof of the restaurant.

The birds of Volcanoes National Park will require many more years of study before we have an adequate understanding of the avifauna in this part of the Virungas. Additional species will no doubt be added to the park's list over time. Every birdwatcher coming to the Virungas needs to bring a pair of binoculars. The park will benefit from all serious efforts to find and report bird sightings.

When I worked at Big Bend National Park in Texas birdwatchers were and still are very important to the understanding of the parks wildlife. The park was established in 1944 and at the time the bird checklist numbered fewer than 100 species. Today park rangers boast of a list of more than 450 species. Big Bend is a birdwatcher's paradise, but if it wasn't for all the park visitors reporting their sightings over the years, park staff would know only half of what they know today.

I hope that including a current list of the birds to Volcanoes National Park in the Appendix will encourage birdwatchers to report their sightings. Birds classified as uncommon may actually turn out to be common. Some species listed as common may turn out to be rare.

Crowned Crane.

Birds of of Volcanoes National Park

Nearly 1,500 species of resident birds have been identified in Africa living in the forests, savannas and deserts south of the Sahara. Many are Old World species familiar to birdwatchers in Europe because of migration routes between the two continents. Some African species like the Ostrich and Cattle Egret are well known. Others, like the park's Handsome Francolin, Ruwenzoni Turaco and Chubb's Cisticola are known only to serious birders.

In February of 2004 a bird survey of the Virungas was undertaken by a team of biologists working on a biological survey conducted by the Wildlife Conservation Society (WCS), Dian Fossey Gorilla Fund International (DFGFI), Institut Congolais pour la Conservation (ICCN), The Rwanda Development Board (RDB), Uganda Wildlife Authority (UWA), Institute of Tropical Forest Conservation (ITFC) and the International Gorilla Conservation Program (IGCP). The team visited 527 locations in the Virungas and found 176 species over a 23 day period. Previously wildlife biologists working in the region had compiled a list of over 700 bird species for all of the Virungas. During the survey 36 new species were identified bringing the total list of birds for the transboundary Virungas protected area to 294 species. At Volcanoes National Park researchers have thus far identified 184 species representing 46 bird families. A complete bird list is included in the Appendix.

At least four park birds are listed by the International Union for the Conservation of Nature (IUCN) as either endangered, vulnerable or near threatened. Other species will no doubt be added to this list as more information becomes available. Grauer's Scrub-warbler (*Bradypterus graueri*), despite being locally common, is threatened because of fragmented habitat across its range in Rwanda, Burundi, DRC and south-western Uganda. In Rwanda, it occurs mainly in the marshes of Rugezi Swamp between the park and Nyungwe Forest. The swamp is not protected and birds are in peril because of encroachment from agriculture and the burning and cutting of vegetation during the dry season.

The rarely seen Lesser Kestrel (*Falco naumanni*) winters in Rwanda and other parts of Africa. This Kestrel is very similar to the Common Kestrel where they occur together from the Mediterranean to Asia. Lessers winter in East and South Africa where flocks of thousands of birds have been observed feeding on grasshoppers. This beautiful falcon is losing its breeding habitat in Europe and Asia and the western European population has declined by 95% since 1950.

Shelley's Crimson-wing (*Cryptospiza shelleyi*) is listed by the IUCN as vulnerable, meaning that population numbers have decreased to a point where the species could become threatened if environmental conditions continue to decline. In the park it is found at elevations between 2,200-3,000 m where it is rarely seen and shows unexplained fluctuations in abundance. It inhabits the understory of closed-canopy moist forest and forest clearings and glades dominated by large herbs and bamboo thickets.

The Kivu Ground-thrush (*Zoothera tanganjicae*) is found at altitudes of 1,500-2,900 m. The overall size of this bird's range is small enough to cause concern. It is listed by the IUCN as vulnerable because of overall habitat loss in the region. Careful monitoring of the population is important to the species long term survival.

Some of the more common birds in the park are goldfinches, crossbills, sunbirds and waxbills. On the edge of the park, watch for the African Citril, common in small flocks, and the Yellow-crowned Canary. When hiking through the Bamboo Zone look for the rather shy Thick-billed Seed-eater and the Streaky Seed-eater. Also on the edge of the park and in the Bamboo Zone you may be able to find the commonly seen Fiscal Shrike. The sharply colored Mackinnon's Shrike with a white V pattern on the back is also seen in this zone.

As you approach the park watch for sunbirds perching on flower stalks along the forest edge like the Bronze Sunbird, Malachite Sunbird and Blue-headed Sunbird. The Blue-headed Sunbird is an endemic species in the Albertine Rift where in the Virungas it is restricted to the lower elevations. When looking for birds in the lower elevation forest and on up into the Hagenia forest look for the uncommon Dusky Crimsonwing, another endemic species.

If you hike into the higher elevations of the Hagenia forest look for the Black-headed Waxbill, Ruwenzoni Turaco, Stripe-breasted Tit, Handsome Francolin, Cardinal Woodpecker, Olive Woodpecker, Strange Weaver and Stuhlmann's Baglafecht Weaver. The remarkably colorful Ruwenzoni Turaco is definitely a prize bird sighting for anyone hiking in the park. Ruwenzonis' have glossy green-blue crests, orange yellow eye-rings, black-blue chins and a maroon throat. Turacos spend all of their time in trees where they feed on fruits while moving in slow noisy flocks.

Bird watching is one of the world's most popular outdoor activities. In Rwanda you will see travelers with binoculars and bird identification field guides, but most have come to see the gorillas, primates at Nyungwe National Park or large animals at Akagera National Park. When visiting Volcanoes National Park your best opportunities to look for birds will be outside your hotel or lodge and on special trips you plan to places like Karisoke, on golden monkey treks and on adventurous climbs to the tops of the volcanoes. As all birdwatchers know, when you go out looking for birds you also have a better chance of seeing other kinds of animals like large and small mammals and reptiles.

Birdwatchers appreciate bird lists at travel destinations around the world. The brief notes on common birds that follow and the complete list included in the Appendix were compiled by researchers working for the Karisoke Research Center. The park and the author would be grateful if you would email bird observation reports to: ricklobello@gmail.com and to DFGFI and RDB by using the contact information on their respective websites.

If you are not an experienced birdwatcher capable of identifying hard-to-find birds like those hiding in dense vegetation, you may find it difficult to identify many of the species you encounter on your gorilla trek. There simply is not enough time to stop and look, and most of your companions will not be interested in waiting for you to identify a bird. As you stop along the way during your steep climb up the mountain you may also be more concerned about catching your breath. Be that as it may, if you invest some of your time preparing to see some of the park's birds a head of time, your trip to the park will be much more memorable as you get to know some of the other fascinating creatures of the Virungas.

On my hike to Karisoke we encountered Yellow-Whiskered Greenbuls. Fortunately my guide was familiar with the bird's song, helping him to identify the species in the dense vegetation. A new e-Guide to the Birds of East Africa designed for iPad, iPhone and iPad Touch includes an extensive set of recordings and is now available on iTunes. Before you pack your bags spend time studying the more common birds of the park by listening to calls and songs. I highly recommend the field guide *Birds of East Africa: Kenya, Tanzania, Uganda, Rwanda and Burundi* by Stevenson and Fanshawe.

In preparing the notes on common birds below I relied heavily on the Karisoke Research Center's wildlife database. When hiking in the park ask your guide if he knows the birds and take notes as you walk along. On a recent birding trip to the abandoned Karisoke camp, my park guides were more familiar with the scientific names (Latin) than the common names. I have included both names in the Appendix. To help increase our understanding of the parks avifauna please report your bird observations while visting the park to the author at ricklobello@gmail.com.

Common Birds of Volcanoes National Park

A complete bird list is included in the Appendix.

Mountain Buzzard, *Buteo oroephilus*
Habitat/Notes: Forested areas of the park.

Common buzzard or European buzzard, *Buteo buteo*
Habitat/Notes: Common winter visitor in the region.

Black Kite, *Milvus migrans*
Habitat/Notes: Widespread throughout the country and one of the most common raptors in the world, Black Kites are commonly seen soaring near developed areas where they have learned to scavenge. Birds may be seen in large flocks.

Handsome Francolin, *Francolinus nobilis*
Habitat/Notes: Widespread, but difficult to see, Handsome Francolins occur in overgrown glades in the Bamboo Zone, in secondary thickets and in Hagenia forest at all levels. This species has also been heard in the Subalpine Zone on Karisimbi at 11,155 ft (3400 m).

Rameron Pigeon or Olive Pigeon
Species: *Columba arquatrix*
Habitat/Notes: Flocks are common throughout Hagenia woodland and numbers of birds may be seen together on fruiting trees. They are hard to see during the day and far more conspicuous in the early morning and evening.

Tambourine Dove
Species: *Turtur tympanistria*
Habitat/Notes: Tambourine Doves are found in the lower elevations of the park.

Handsome Francolin.

Ruwenzoni Turaco, *Tauraco /Ruwenzorornis johnstoni*
Habitat/Notes: The Ruwenzoni Turaco is found throughout the Hagenia forest ranging into Hypericum thickets and the Subalpine Zone to 11,811 ft (3600 m).

Montane Nightjar, *Caprimulgus ruwenzorii*
Habitat/Notes: Nightjars are common and widespread in highland areas between 4,921-9,843 ft (1500-3000 m). Watch for them around the foot of Sabyinyo and Gahinga Volcanoes.

Mottled Swift, *Tachymarptis aequatorialis*
Habitat/Notes: This bird prefers the higher elevations of the park, but can also be seen feeding over wetland areas.

Speckled Mousebird, *Colius striatus*
Habitat/Notes: Small flocks of Mousebirds are widespread and common in a variety of moister bush areas from thickets to forest edges. They are commonly seen in small groups of secondary thickets up to 9,514 ft (2900 m), but less common in open Hagenia Forest.

European Bee-eater, *Merops apiaster*
Habitat/Notes: Bee-eaters are abundant migrants in open areas from the end of August to November. Watch for them near bee nests maintained by local beekeepers.

Crowned Hornbill, *Tockus alboterminatus*
Habitat/Notes: Watch for hornbills almost anywhere in the forest especially along the forest edge.

Yellow-rumped Tinkerbird, *Pogoniulus bilineatus*
Habitat/Notes: Tinkerbirds can be found throughout the forest.

Olive Woodpecker, *Dendropicos Mesopicos / griseocephalus*
Habitat/Notes: Olive Woodpeckers are found throughout the Ficalhoa and Hagenia forest to 10,499 ft (3200 m).

Black Saw-wing, *Psalidoprocne holomelas*
Habitat/Notes: These swallows are often seen hawking over secondary thickets and forests up to 9,514 ft (2900 m).

Cinnamon-chested Bee-Eater.

African Sandmartin / Plain Martin, *Riparia paludicola*
Habitat/Notes: African Sandmartins breed at the Bisoke trailhead between June and October. They are often seen hawking over open spaces such as secondary thickets, agricultural land and marshy meadows.

Richard's Pipit, *Anthus anthus*
Habitat/Notes: Look for Richard's Pipits in agricultural fields surrounding the park.

Donherty's Bushshrike, *Lanius mackinnoni*
Habitat/Notes: Donherty's Bushshrikes are reasonably common, but shy and difficult to observe in the undergrowth of highland forests from 5,249-11,483 ft (1600-3500 m). They are most common on Sabyinyo and Gahinga.

Mackinnon's Grey Shrike, *Lanius collaris*
Habitat/Notes: Mackinnon's Grey Shrikes have been recorded up to 8,858 ft (2700 m) in secondary thicket, scrub bamboo and agricultural areas on the edge of the park.

Ladgen's Bush-Shrike, *Malacanotus lagdeni*
Habitat/Notes: The park is one of the best places in Africa to see this species. It has been seen at elevations up to 9,514 ft (2900 m) in open Hagenia woodland, secondary thicket and Hypericum thicket.

Cape Robin Chat, *Cossypha caffra*
Habitat/Notes: Cape Robin Chats are most often seen in secondary thickets around the edge of the park. They are also found in the Subalpine Zone on Karisimbi at 11,483 ft (3500m). In recent years a breeding pair has been seen in the Bisoke parking area.

Stone Chat or African Stonechat, *Saxicola torquata*
Habitat/Notes: Stone Chats can be seen in a variety of areas around the park up to 8,202 ft (2500 m). Look for them in open areas and on fence posts.

White-starred Bush Robin, *Pogonocichla stellata*
Habitat/Notes: Easily overlooked Bush Robins are widespread in the understory of the Hagenia forest up to 10,171 ft (3100 m) and one of the commoner birds of dense bamboo, Ficalhoa forest and secondary thicket. Park birds lack the white star on the upper breast making them a challenge to identify for many birdwatchers.

Olive Thrush, *Turdus olivaceus*
Habitat/Notes: This common bird lives in the understory of secondary thickets and Hagenia woodland up to 10,499 ft (3200 m).

Archer's Robin-Chat, *Dessonornis archeri*
Habitat/Notes: The ground foraging Archer's Robin-Chat rarely leaves the shelter of dense undergrowth and is found from the edge of the park up to the Subalpine Zone at 11,811 ft (3600 m). It is most abundant in Hagenia and Ficalhoa forest.

Abyssinian Hill Babbler, *Alcippe/ Pseudoalcippe abyssinica*
Habitat/Notes: These babblers are most common in Hagenia forest with dense understory. They also occur in secondary thickets and Ficalhoa forest. Birds are occasionally seen associated with mixed groups of other species where they range up to 9,514 ft (2900 m).

Chestnut-Throated Apalis, *Apalis porphyrolaema*
Habitat/Notes: The Chestnut-throated Apalis is found in relict Ficalhoa forest, Hagenia forest and relict trees in secondary thicket up to 9,843 ft (3000 m). A forest canopy species, it is found in small groups and often with mixed groups of other species.

Wing-Snapping Cistcola, *Cisticola ayersii*
Habitat/Notes: Wing-Snapping Cisticolas inhabits open grasslands and cultivated areas near the edge of the park up to 8,530 ft (2600 m).

Chubb's Cisticola, *Cisticola chubbi*
Habitat/Notes: Chubb's Cisticolas are found in secondary thicket, scrub bamboo, Hagenia forest and Ficalhoa forest. They are usually found in small groups in thickets and scrub bamboo decreasing in abundance with increasing altitude up to 10,499 ft (3200 m).

Red-faced Woodland Warbler, *Phylloscopus laetus*
Habitat/Notes: Red-faced Woodland Warblers are found in Ficalhoa forest, Hagenia forest and secondary thickets close to the forest edge. They are often associated with groups of mixed species.

Brown Woodland Warbler, *Phylloscopus umbrovirens*
Habitat/Notes: Brown Woodland Warblers are most common in Hagenia forest, Hypericum thickets and the lower Subalpine Zone. They are often found in mixed groups of other species and appear to be strongly associated with areas dominated by Hypericum and *Erica arborescens*.

White-eyed Slaty Flycatcher, *Melaenornis fischeri*
Habitat/Notes: White-eyed Slaty Flycatchers are found up to 10,499 ft (3200 m), most commonly in Hagenia forest, but also in secondary thickets and Ficalhoa forest.

Pied Flycatcher, *Ficedula hypoleuca*
Habitat/Notes: Pied Flycatchers have been found at elevations up to 9,514 ft (2900 m) in all habitats, although they are uncommon in bamboo.

Chin-spot Puff-Backed Flycatcher or Chinspot, *Batis molitor*
Habitat/Notes: Chin-spots are common in forest and bamboo. They are generally easy to observe and are also found in secondary thickets and forested habitats up to 9,843 ft (3000 m).

Mountain Yellow (Warbler) Flycatcher, *Chloropeta similis*
Habitat/Notes: Mountain Yellow Flycatchers are found in secondary thickets, Ficalhoa forest and Hagenia forest up to 10,499 ft (3200 m).

Paradise Flycatcher, *Phyllomyias griseiceps*
Habitat/Notes: Paradise Flycatchers are seen with regularity in Hagenia and Ficalhoa forest up to 600m where they are found in dense understory vegetation. There is also record of a bird in the dense crown of an isolated *Hypericum* in secondary thicket at 9,186 ft (2800 m).

Stripe-breasted Tit, *Parus fasciiventer*
Habitat/Notes: Stripe-breasted Tits are common in Hagenia and Ficalhoa forest and in secondary thickets close to the forest edge and in Hypericum thickets up to 10,827 ft (3300 m). They are also often seen in mixed species groups.

Yellow-whiskered Greenbul (Bulbul), *Andropadus latirostris*
Habitat/Notes: Yellow-whiskered Greenbuls are restricted to Ficalhoa and secondary forest on Sabyinyo and Gahinga.

Common Bulbul, *Pycnonotus barbatus*
Habitat/Notes: Common Bulbuls are extremely common and widespread up to 9,843 ft (3000 m). They are found in Ficalhoa forest, secondary thickets and Hagenia forest.

Regal Sunbird, *Cinnyris regia*
Habitat/Notes: Regal Sunbirds are common in bamboo and often seen in Ficalhoa forest, secondary thickets and lower Hagenia forest.

Scarlet-Tufted Malachite Sunbird, *Nectarinia johnstoni*
Habitat/Notes: Scarlet-Tufted Malachite Sunbirds are abundant in the Subalpine Zone between 11,811- 13,123 ft (3600 and 4000 m), especially where stands of giant Lobelia are in flower. Birds will descend to the marshy meadows and Hagenia forest of the Karisimbi-Bisoke saddle.

African Citril, *Serinus citrinelloides*
Habitat/Notes: African Citrils are common is small flocks where they are found at the forest edge, in moist scrub, gardens and cultivated areas. They can be seen in agricultural areas, secondary thickets and Hagenia forest. They are often associated with thistles.

Yellow-Crowned Canary or Cape Canary, *Serinus canicollis*
Habitat/Notes: The Yellow-Crowned Canary is common in the agricultural areas bordering the park and within the park up to 9,186 ft (2800m). Small flocks enter the forest primarily to feed on Hagenia seeds.

Crested Eagle.

Streaky Seed-Eater, *Serinus striolatus*
Habitat/Notes: Streaky Seed-Eaters are very common in agricultural areas, secondary thickets, scrub bamboo, Hagenia forest and open meadows and at 12,467 ft (3800 m) in the Subalpine Zone.

Brimstone Canary, *Serinus sulphuratus*
Habitat/Notes: The Brimstone Canary is found in pairs or as single birds in cultivated areas and secondary thickets up to 7,874 ft (2400 m).

Black-Headed Waxbill, *Estrilda atricapilla*
Habitat/Notes: Small flocks of Black-Headed Waxbills are abundant in agricultural areas, secondary thickets and Hagenia woodland.

Black-Crowned Waxbill, *Estrilda nonnula*
Habitat/Notes: Black-Crowned Waxbills are common at the forest edge, in secondary growth, marshy and cultivated areas.

Yellow-Bellied Waxbill, *Estrilda quartinia*
Habitat/Notes: Yellow-Bellied Waxbills are common at the forest edge, in highland grasslands and around cultivated areas.

Sooty Chat, *Myrmecocichla nigra*

Habitat/Notes: Sooty Chats inhabit open cultivated areas and pastures on the park edge above Kinigi, Gasiza and on the eastern slopes of Muhabura up to 8,202 ft (2500 m).

Strange Weaver, *Ploceus alienus*

Habitat/Notes: The Strange Weaver is primarily a bird of Hagenia and Ficalhoa forest where they have been recorded up to 10,499 ft (3200 m). Birds are often associated with mixed bird species, but generally keep to the undergrowth where they are usually seen foraging in withered leaves hanging from the bushes.

Stuhlmann's Baglafecht Weaver, *Ploceus baglafecht*

Habitat/Notes: Stuhlmann's Baglafecht Weavers are common in the agricultural areas bordering the park and less frequently in secondary thickets and Hagenia woodland.

Yellow-Billed Oxpecker, *Buphagus africanus*

Habitat/Notes: Yellow-Billed Oxpeckers typically occur in small loose flocks where they feed near a variety of large mammals.

White-Necked Raven, *Corvus albicollis*

Habitat/Notes: White-Necked Ravens are common in agriculture areas and throughout the park up to the summit of Karisimbi and are attracted to camp sites. Fossey wrote about "two delightfully mischievous" ravens at Kabara Meadow that eventually learned to unzip her tent to get at food.

Pied Crow, *Corvus albus*

Habitat/Notes: Pied Crows are common in agriculture areas around the park and are often seen at tourist accommodations like the Gorilla's Nest Lodge.

Pied Crows.

Young bushbuck.

Guide to Rwanda's Volcanoes National Park

All around the world people are fascinated with the animals of Africa. The continent has many of our favorites including the big five, the most sought after animals everyone on safari wants to see: elephants, rhinos, buffaloes, lions and leopards. Other safari favorites include crocodiles, ostriches, cheetahs, wild dogs, antelope, zebras, giraffes, chimpanzees and gorillas. Birdwatchers come too, and if you have avid birders in your group you'll learn about many more species than you ever imagined. Volcanoes National Park has only two big five species, the forest buffalo and forest elephant, and very few visitors ever see more than their tracks and droppings because of all the dense forest vegetation. To see the big five and other large animals you'll need to make plans to visit other parks. In Rwanda you can see most of big five animals at Akagera National Park. Other well-known parks in the region for big five animals include Queen Elizabeth National Park in Uganda, Masai Mara in Kenya and Serengeti National Park in Tanzania.

On a recent trip up the side of Mt. Sabyinyo my group hiked nearly two hours before we found the gorillas. Along the way we heard birds and found buffalo tracks, but little else until we came across a beautiful bushbuck down in a side ravine. About the size of a small deer in the United States, its light reddish brown coat glistened in the sunshine against the bright green vegetation. On our way back we saw a tree squirrel, a chameleon and some golden monkeys.

To get to know the mammals of this mountain park the same rules must be followed as in other parts of the world. You need to spend more than a day, and at Volcanoes National Park that means making plans to go on special tours organized by RDB. Bushbuck, duiker and golden monkeys are going to be your best possibilities. There will be chances to see other species, but you will need some luck and perseverance since finding many requires being in the right place at the right time.

Golden monkey.

Mammals of Volcanoes National Park

Biological surveys of Volcanoes National Park conducted in 2003 and 2004 documented the presence of elephant, bushbuck, blue duiker, forest buffalo, giant forest hog, mountain gorilla, golden monkey, blue and L'Hoest's monkey and hyrax. The 2004 survey focused mainly on plants and birds while the 2003 survey was organized to census the mountain gorillas. If more time had been spent looking for smaller mammals like rodents and shrews many more species could have been found.

Research on mammals at Volcanoes National Park has focused largely on mountain gorillas, golden monkeys and forest buffalo. Most of what is known comes from the writings of Karisoke researchers, a database maintained by the Karisoke Research

Center and notes that Fossey and Schaller included in their books. Many of the park's larger mammals are rarely seen because they are found in small numbers, are secretive in nature or are nocturnal. Increased park patrols and a rock wall border fence on the eastern boundary have helped to decrease the impact of poaching, but the overall impact of humans on the park's mammal species has not been adequately studied.

Predators like leopards were eradicated long ago. Smaller cats like golden cats and servals are present, but today humans are the number one large predator of the Virungas. Other mammalian predators in the Virunga ecosystem include jackals, mongooses, civets, honey badgers, zorillas and hyenas.

One of the more commonly encountered large animals is the bushbuck (*Tragelaphus scriptus*), which inhabits dense vegetation near water. These spiral horned antelopes are related to the sitatunga, nyla, lesser kudu and eland. Another close relative, the bongo (*Boocerus euryceros*), is nearly three times the size of the bushbuck. Bongos are the largest of the forest antelopes and extremely rare. Most records of this beautiful striped ungulate are from the DRC side of the Virungas where it was recently reported for the first time in almost 50 years.

Five of Africa's seventeen species of duikers are known to the park. Little information is available on exactly where these different antelope species live, but some species in the park appear to be more abundant than others. With the exception of the yellow-backed duiker that grows as big as a bushbuck, most of the duikers are smaller, weighing less than 50 pounds.

Blue duikers (*Cephalophus monticola*) are tiny compared to other antelope species. They stand a little over a foot tall and weigh from 8.4 to 12 pounds. All across West Africa blue duikers are common where they are a mainstay of the bushmeat trade. Because of their small size they are rarely seen. As you wander through the park watch for the up and down movements of their white tails. If you are very lucky a moving tail might help you find one.

The black-fronted duiker (*Cephalophus nigrifrons*) prefers lowland areas over most of its range in Central Africa, but in the Virungas it is found at altitudes of up to 10,499 ft (3200m) where the vegetation changes to small shrubs and succulents. They live in pairs, sometimes with a third individual believed to be offspring. Like the blue duiker they are diurnal making it possible to see one as you walk through the forest.

Rare black fronted duiker (Cephalophus nigrifrons).

One animal that may have lived in the park area before the lower elevation areas were converted to agriculture is the okapi. These secretive deep forest ungulates of the DRC are highly unusual in their appearance, looking like a cross between a giraffe and an antelope. An okapi was recently documented at nearby Virunga National Park, but the natural recovery of the species is threatened by poaching and political unrest.

The largest hoofed mammal in the park is the forest buffalo (*Syncerus caffer nanus*). Visitors often come across sign of buffalo including droppings and tracks. They are shy and rarely seen and unlike buffalo living on the savannas, the ones in the forest live in much smaller groups. The rock wall border fence deters movement of buffalo, but does not prevent it. For example, in May of 2007 twenty forest buffaloes wandered out of the park to raid crops, and farmers soon killed thirteen of them. Park staff tried to assist the people affected by helping to chase the animals back into the park, but the people refused, saying that they needed to be compensated for the crops they lost and that killing the animals was justified.

Some species of large mammals are present in very low densities. Still others not believed to be present in the Rwanda section of the transboundary area could move into the park from the DRC and Uganda. For example, African elephants believed by some to be forest elephants may actually be elephants roaming into the park from grassland areas in Virunga National Park. There appears to be adequate habitat for elephants in Volcanoes National Park, but without the cooperation of the people living nearby it is doubtful that a sustainable population can be protected. One way an elephant population might be restored to this part of Rwanda would be to gain the cooperation of people living in nearby shambas (farms) to support elephant conservation as a way to increase tourism. For that support to be realized, however, agricultural areas would need to be protected from elephants that wander outside the park. This would be a big challenge, but may be possible if elephant control measures like planting chili peppers are established and if increased revenues from park fees are directed to benefit the local community.

An important discovery in the Zambezi Valley showed that elephants are sensitive to capsaicin, that part of the chili pepper causing the hot taste. Elephants hate chili and can be controlled and kept from agricultural areas by erecting chili fences, coating posts and rails with chili and burning chili briquettes.

Restoring leopards to the park would much more difficult. Leopards prey on livestock and can also prey upon humans and gorillas. Park managers should still look into the possibility since it is very possible that the Virunga ecosystem needs leopards to keep ungulates like antelope and buffalo in check. An unchecked ungulate population could someday threaten the gorilla food supply. Little is known about how the return leopards would impact the Virunga ecosytem.

In addition to gorillas smaller primates inhabiting the Virungas include golden monkeys, blue monkeys and L'Hoest's monkeys. The golden monkey is one of the rarest of a group of monkeys called guenons. There are twenty-six species of guenons in Africa. They are colorful, medium sized primates that spend most of their time in trees.

Golden monkeys are limited to three areas of critical habitat: the Virunga transboundary protected area, Rwanda's Nyungwe forest and the Gishwati forest. DFGFI and RDB park staff have been working to habituate part of the park's golden monkey population to help further develop Rwanda's expanding ecotourism industry. It is hoped that revenues generated by golden monkey treks combined with other park related fees, will help Rwanda maintain its status as one of the top tourist destinations in equatorial Africa. Funds generated from ecotourism are essential to the country's economy and overall conservation efforts.

Golden monkeys spend most of their time in the Bamboo Zone eating flowers, fruits, insects and bamboo leaves. Bamboo makes up the bulk of their diet and their preference for this lower elevation plant zone helps to ensure the success of golden monkey guided treks. They live in large family groups of up to 64 individuals with a dominant male as the leader. In 2011 researchers counted 3,498 individuals living in 265 groups, a decline from nearly 5,000 individuals counted in 2007.

Bats and rodents make up about 50% of the 137 mammal species listed in the Karisoke database included in the Appendix. When you add eighteen species of moles and shrews on the list, it is easy to understand why so many mammal species are difficult to find because of their small size and nocturnal habits.

The park's mammal list helps to paint a picture of what can be expected in the Virungas, but does little to explain how most of the mammal species are faring. More research is needed to adequately understand the park's biodiversity. Increased research funding plus funding for comprehensive environmental education programs and poaching patrols are critical to the long term protection of the ecosystem.

Gorilla and other ecotourism initiatives are important to the park because they help to support research and conservation. Corresponding publicity helps non-profit organizations with their fundraising efforts in support of research, conservation and socio-economic programs. One of the best ways visitors can support park conservation efforts is through membership in the Dian Fossey Gorilla Fund International (www.gorillafund.org).

The species profiles that follow provide an overview of what is known about some of the park's other species of mammals. To help increase our understanding of the park please report mammal sightings you make to the author at ricklobello@gmail.com.

Other Mammals of Volcanoes National Park

A complete mammal list is included in the Appendix.

Northern giant musk shrew, *Crocidura olivieri*
Special Notes: There may be more species of mammals in the genus *Crocidura* than any other genus in the park. All across Africa biologists have described 106 species and it is likely that more species await discovery. The musk shrew weighs only up to 2.8 ounces (78 grams). Shrews like the musk shrew are active during both daylight and nighttime hours and may be encountered in a wide variety of niches including abandoned burrows, hollow trees and rock crevices. When you walk through the forest take a moment to glance into the thick vegetation, you might just be fortunate enough to catch a glimpse of one of the park's fifteen species of shrews.

Rousette fruit bat, *Rousettus lanosus*
Special Notes: Many of the bats in the area are fruit eating bats. Since most fruit eating bats are active during the day, you are more likely to see them than the nocturnal species that feed on insects. Look for rousette fruit bats in the palm trees along the shores of Lake Kivu at Rubavu. Fruit bats are very important to the dispersal of seeds and pollination in rainforests. In fact, in areas where the rainforest is allowed to regenerate from fire and the impacts of humans, fruit and nectar eating bats play an important role in restoring plant diversity.

Bosman's Potto, *Peridictcus potto*
Special Notes: Four species of bushbabies are known to the Virungas including Bosman's potto which has been recorded at the Karisoke Research Center. Pottos are nocturnal slow moving primates that spend most of their time in the trees. Very little is known about them in the wild.

Fruit bats.

Blue monkey, *Cercopithecus mitis stuhlmanni*
Special Notes: Fossey had a pet blue monkey named Kima at her Karisoke Camp. She acquired the monkey from a man in Rubavu about an hour's drive east of the park. This species does not appear on the Karisoke database, but is noted as a possible park species by others. It has been reported at Mgahinga Gorilla National Park in the northwest quadrant of the Virungas.

Forest Pouched Rat, *Cricetomys gambianus*
Special Notes: Fossey enjoyed watching a family of pouched rats she discovered feeding on her left-over corn supply. They soon reproduced to a point where rats inhabited every building in camp. She eventually decided that they were no longer welcome and they all moved away after she deprived them of their food supply.

Pouched rats are nocturnal, but are also occasionally seen during the day when they behave as if they are almost blind, sitting up and sniffing the air in all directions.

Leopard, *Panthera pardus*
Local Name: Ingwe
Special Notes: On Christmas Day 1978 Karisoke staff reported a leopard sighting less than a mile away from camp. Earlier that year they found leopard scat in a nearby cave, but outside of those accounts there are few written records of leopards for the park. A recent UNESCO report states that there are leopards in the northwest sector of the Virungas at Mgahinga Gorilla National Park.

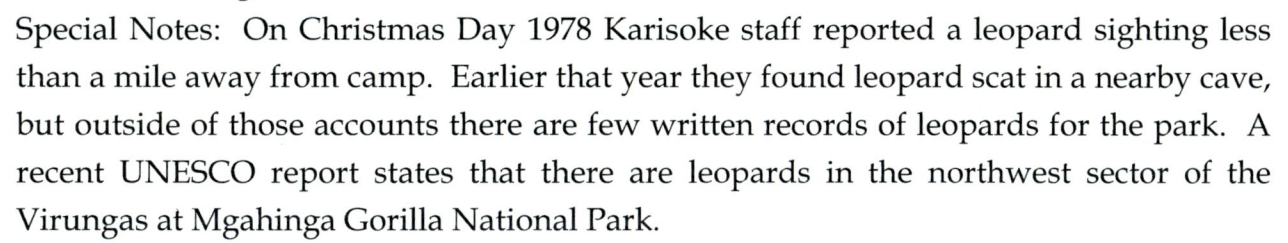

Spotted hyena, *Crocuta crocuta*
Local Name: Impyisi
Special Notes: Karisoke staff reported a large and active population of hyenas in the Virungas on Sabyinyo's eastern slope in 1978. Because it is very unusual for hyenas to inhabit forested areas, one can speculate that hyenas in the Virungas have adapted to the loss of open habitat on the park's eastern boundary by seeking refuge in the forest during the day.

Serval, *Felis serval*
Local Name: Imondo
Special Notes: Servals have been reported in the park in the Subalpine Zone. These small spotted cats with long legs prefer savanna habitat and are known to inhabit the northwestern sector of the Virungas at Mgahinga Gorilla National Park.

African golden cat, *Profelis aurata*
Special Notes: This small cat has been reported from the Bamboo Zone of the park and at Mgahinga Gorilla National Park. Golden cats inhabit tropical forests across Africa. Because the population size across its entire range is estimated at below 10,000 mature breeding individuals, with a declining trend due to habitat and prey base loss and poaching, the IUCN lists this species as vulnerable.

MAMMALS OF VOLCANOES NATIONAL PARK

White-faced bush pig, *Potamochoerus larvatus hassama*
Special Notes: Bush pigs are found in the dense vegetation of high elevation forests. They are nocturnal and forage in groups of up to twenty animals uncovering roots, insects and other food items they push up from the forest floor. White-faced bush pigs and red river hogs potentially compete with gorillas for food. Fortunately for the forest, their intense rooting does not normally seriously damage the plants on which they feed.

Red River hog, African bush pig, *Potamochoerus porcus*
Local Name: Ingurube y'ishyamaba
Special Notes: This species of bush pig is widespread and abundant in lower elevation forests of the DRC, Rwanda and Burundi in what appears to be an ecologically/attitudinally separated relationship with the white-faced bushpig of the higher elevations. Fossey reported how her staff remembered bush pigs as being numerous when parkland was being taken for cultivation in 1967.

Giant forest hog, *Hylochoerus meinertzhageni meinertzhageni (schultzi)*.
Local Names: Isenge
Special Notes: During her first few months in the Virungas Fossey described watching a giant forest hog in Kabara Meadow for about an hour thinking the movements in the dense vegetation were of a mountain gorilla. Several days later she found the animal lying dead under a Hagenia tree. Weighing up to 600 pounds (275 kg) and standing up to 3.5 feet (1100 mm) at the shoulders, these formidable creatures are the largest members of the pig family. They are rarely seen in the park, but are found in dense forests across equatorial Africa.

Red river hog.

Tree hyrax, *Dendrohydrax arboreus*
Special Notes: Fossey heard tree hyraxes making "squeaky door-screech choruses" from her Karisoke cabin. Bill Weber described the sounds of tree hyraxes at night as creating "unearthly crescendos of sleep-defying screams." Tree hyraxes prefer lower elevations in the forest where they take shelter in tree holes and dense vegetation. They forage in the upper forest canopy where they feed on leaves, fruits, twigs and bark.

Tree hyrax.

Guide to Rwanda's Volcanoes National Park

Ask your park guide to find you a chameleon. They are very common, but difficult to find. Exquisitely camouflaged among the branches of trees and shrubs, both people and gorillas find that chameleons are interesting to look at.

Most travelers to Rwanda are most interested in seeing large mammals and birds, but these larger and more easily seen species account for a very small percentage of the species richness in the Virungas. Most of the animals in the park are of the smaller kind including thousands of yet-to-be-discovered species of invertebrates like insects, spiders and millipedes. Few people visiting Volcanoes National Park have seen or have paid much attention to these creatures, yet they are everywhere, inhabiting all conceivable niches in the rocks, soil and vegetation.

For those who are curious to know what other species have been recorded the park, the Karisoke Research Center has compiled a list of reptiles and amphibians (Appendix). Research projects that focus on small animals and invertebrates are lacking and need to be conducted throughout the Virungas to help come up with a more clearer picture of the area's biodiversity. When that happens, knowledge of the park's animals and plants will increase dramatically and we will have a more complete understanding of the Virunga ecosystem than we do today.

Chameleon on a eucalyptus branch.

Other Animals of Volcanoes National Park

When you visit the park finding small animals is not as easy as it might seem. Many are hiding in the thick vegetation and active only at night while others, being cold blooded, are active only during the warmer part of the day. The Karisoke database of reptiles and amphibians lists eight species of snakes, eleven species of lizards and eleven species of frogs. Six of the eleven lizard species are chameleons, a mainly Old World group of lizards with prehensile tails. A complete list of reptiles and amphibians known to the park is included in the Appendix.

Chameleons are well known for their ability to change colors. If it weren't for the experienced eyes of trackers and guides most people would never see them. They blend in with their surroundings almost perfectly. The Karisoke reptile list includes: Elliot's chameleon, three-horned chameleon, coarse chameleon, Boulenger's pygmy chameleon, striped chameleon and flap-neck chameleon. These tree dwelling lizards are known mainly to Africa where 89 of the 93 chameleon species live. Nearly 50% of Africa's chameleon species live on the island of Madagascar. Of the 19 reptile species known to inhabit the park, chameleons make up 32% of the reptilian fauna. Other lizards include three species of skink, a tree lizard called the sparse-scaled forest lizard and a gecko.

The cooler temperatures of this high elevation rainforest make it easy to understand why so few species of cold-blooded reptiles are present. In contrast, the much larger Virunga National Park in the DRC, with its wider variety of warmer low elevation habitats, is home to 109 species of reptiles. What does all this mean to those going to see the gorillas in Rwanda? It means that those who are afraid of snakes have fewer serpentine creatures to worry about.

Turtles are apparently not present in the park although there may be some water turtles living in nearby lakes. Snakes on the other hand are present and there are seven known species: Montane egg-eater snake, forest vine snake, Angola green snake, Rwanda forest green snake, Gunther's green tree snake, rhinoceros-horned viper and Nitshe's bush viper.

Like members of the viper family in the Americas, vipers in the Old World have the characteristic fangs and temperature-sensitive pit organs located on the side of the head between the eye and the nostril. And like the pit vipers in the Americas, they are very dangerous. The rhinoceros-horned viper is a short thick-bodied snake about 4 feet (1.2 m) long that prefers habitats near water and is largely nocturnal. They have hornlike scales at the tip of the snout and are beautifully decorated with blue, black, purple, red and yellow complicated patterns of geometric rhomboidal triangular forms. To avoid running into one remember to be alert and try to avoid walking or reaching into thick vegetation. They are rarely encountered on gorilla treks, but you should always be vigilant when hiking.

Five other forest snakes in the park are members of the Colubrid family, a very large family of snakes (1,500 species) found in both the Old and New World. Gunther's green treesnake, Rwanda forest green snake and large-eyed green treesnake are all members of the subfamily Colubrinae with characteristic slender bodies and no venomous fangs. These snakes are active during the day and night and are most likely to be seen climbing in the trees and bushes.

Most snakes in the park prey upon birds and their eggs; one -- the montane egg-eater snake -- has a reputation for preferring eggs. This non-venomous snake spends most of its time in the trees looking for bird nests. When it eats an egg the contents are squeezed into the stomach and then bits of shell are regurgitated.

Amphibians

Herpetologists who study snakes and lizards are also interested in the study of frogs and toads. Eleven species of amphibians are known to the park including the warty stripe-legged frog, De Witte's clawed frog, montane reed frog, Pitman's common reed frog, Bayon's common reed frog, Karisimbi forest tree frog and the montane golden toad. No other class of vertebrates is as threatened with extinction as are the amphibians. According to the IUCN amphibians are significantly more threatened than other vertebrate groups with 21% of all amphibian species rated as critically endangered or endangered.

One notable endangered species in the park is the little known Karisimbi forest tree frog (*Leptopelis karissimbensis*). Tree frogs in this genus are from the family Hyperoliidae, a group of frogs with the reputation for spending most of their lives in trees. The Karisimbi forest tree frog is listed as endangered because it's estimated range occupies an area of less than 5,000 km^2. All individuals are known from fewer than five locations and there is continuing decline in the extent and quality of its habitat. It occurs throughout the Virungas in all three protected areas.

Fish

Eighty-two species of fish have been found in the fresh water lakes and streams of Rwanda. Most species are from the families Cyprinidae and Cichlidae. One of the most common species encountered at area lakes and restaurants is tilapia, a member of the family Cichlidae and an important protein source across Africa and in Western fish markets.

Fisheries in Rwanda operate mainly at lakes Kivu, Cyohoha and Mugesera. The country is currently working on developing its fishing industry which over time will become a more important source of protein.

Some of the Great Lakes of Africa including lakes in the mountains and ranges of the Virunga-Albertine Rift region are very rich in fish species. As many as 325 species of fish have been found in Lake Tanganyika. But that kind of diversity is apparently not the case near the park. Lake Kivu to the south has recorded only 28 species. Closer by at smaller lakes fed by the park's mountain runoff the known biodiversity of fish is even less. At Lake Bulera, just east of Musanze, the fish diversity is extremely low with only ten species, three of which have been introduced. Overall the fish of this area are poorly understood and where they do occur they are often over exploited. The low species diversity is more of an indicator of the information available in the literature than the true picture of what probably lives in these lakes today.

The situation for fish is not much brighter at nearby Virunga National Park in the DRC. Thirty years ago the world's biggest population of 29,000 hippos at the park fertilized the lakes and streams. Today there are now only about 600 hippos struggling to survive after years of relentless poaching. With so many hippos gone from the ecosystem and a very uncertain future, fish living in the same waters with the hippos will no doubt be adversely affected.

Invertebrates

Invertebrates living in Virunga forests include thousands of species of insects and other taxonomic groups of arthropods including spiders, termites and snails. With the exception of butterflies, animals in this category have been poorly studied in this part of

Mountain gorillas although largely vegetarian will sometimes eat insects and snails.

equatorial Africa even though nearly 100,000 species of insects have been described in sub-Saharan region. Hopefully future teams of zoologists will tackle the park's invertebrate biodiversity, no doubt one of the greatest scientific study challenges in the region and around the world.

To date we know of 117 species of endemic butterflies in the Albertine Rift area with 21 species of endemics in Virunga National Park. One species to look and hope for is the African giant swallowtail butterfly (*Papilio antimachus* DRURY), the largest butterfly of Africa. With a wingspan of nearly 10 inches (25 cm) you would think that spotting one might be easy until you learn that these spectacular flying insects prefer living high in the tree tops. Swallowtail butterflies have very colorful larvae with thoraxes resembling the head of a snake.

Other insects you may encounter include tsetse flies, mosquitoes and dung beetles. There are 21 species of blood sucking tsetse flies in Africa with two species identified as spreading the fatal sleeping sickness through a trypanosomal parasite. Africa has a long history of controlling flies through vegetation clearing, game control and the use of insecticides.

The best way to avoid potentially dangerous species of flies is to stay away from places where there are known infections. Updates on outbreaks are often reported on www.mdtravelhealth.com website and at the World Health Organization website at www.who.int/csr/don/en. You can also help protect yourself by wearing medium weight fabric long sleeves and pants that are neutral in color and blend in with the environment. There is no vaccine to protect you from a potential tsetse fly bite, but you can take a prophylaxis like mefloquine (Lariam), atovaquone/proguanil (Malarone), or doxycycline to help prevent a potential case of malaria.

African giant swallowtail butterfly.

Dian Fossey noted some of the invertebrates that were associated with the gorillas. A cestode parasite called *Anoplocephala gorillae*, a large flatworm, was often found in gorilla dung. She described gorilla nests that seemed alive with the 1 inch (25 mm) long worms.

Although she did not identify them by species Fossey also noted how gorillas will search for larvae and grub matter from within the inner stalks of the parasitic flowering shrub *Loranthus luteo-aurantiacus*. She was impressed with how the two baby gorillas under her care, Coco and Pucker, loved eating grubs so much that they preferred them over special treats like blackberries. Fossey thought that the gorillas might be interested in swarms of termites, like those eaten by chimpanzees and lowland gorillas. In the Virungas studies have shown that mountain gorillas avoid termites, but will occasionally eat ants and the cocoons of unknown invertebrates.

Most people have little appreciation for the tiny creatures of the world. Unfortunately, insects and their kin are looked at more as pests than for the roles they play in helping to maintain ecosystems. If you are a trained entomologist or even thinking about becoming one, perhaps you will consider helping Rwanda better understand this important part of its biodiversity. Conserving the Virunga ecosystem entails understanding all the parts.

After many years reading about the life of Dian Fossey the thought that I would soon visit Karisoke, the site where she launched her monumental gorilla study and lived for many years, was all I needed to get motivated for the steep climb ahead. After spending three days visiting the Susa and Sabyinyo Groups I was psyched.

When we parked our Land Rover at the trailhead I recognized the spot from an old photograph I had seen of Fossey with her Land Rover "Lily". I was very fortunate to be accompanied on the hike by Karisoke Research Center staff Serge Nsengimana, the Education Program Officer and Fidele Uwimana, Field Data Coordinator.

It was a sunny May morning and along our way we spotted a family of about a dozen golden monkeys running into the trees from a potato field at the edge of the park. Thinking that they were seen only on special treks, I hadn't expected to see golden monkeys. Every hike in the park comes with its own surprises.

Everything Fidele had to say about Fossey was of great interest since as a young boy he had worked for her at Karisoke. He stopped at a clearing about 30 minutes from the camp and told the story of how this part of the trail was called the Porter's Trail and how where we were standing was a popular rest stop for Fossey and her porters. He then went on to enthusiastically explain how Fossey came up with the name Karisoke; "When Fossey got here she sees this mountain Visoke and Mt. Karisimbi and she says I have to call my camp Karisoke because it is between Karisimbi and Visoke. Everybody now takes time here."

Hagenia trees growing near Karisoke.

Pied kingfishers on hippos.

Exploring more of the park and beyond the Virungas

After you see the gorillas there is much more to discover in the land of a thousand hills. When making your safari travel plans consider spending your entire vacation in Rwanda -- a very practical idea if you are considering a one or two-week trip. If you have just one week your itinerary could include four days exploring Volcanoes National Park visiting the gorillas, golden monkeys and Dian Fossey's Karisoke research camp and three days exploring the savanna at Akagera National Park. If you have two weeks tack on two or three days looking for chimpanzees and other primates at Nyungwe National Park, two to three days visiting the capital city of Kigali, memorial sites and the National Museum at Butare and the rest of your second week exploring Akagera. Depending on your interests you can also swing on over to Queen Elizabeth National Park in Uganda. Arrange for a tour company specializing in Rwanda and let them know what you want to do. If possible I recommend that you spend three days with the gorillas. Gorilla trek permits are now $750 per day and well worth the money when you consider how almost every dollar is earmarked for conservation and socio-economic projects near the park.

More to see at Volcanoes National Park

Karisoke Research Camp

A growing number of people coming to see the gorillas spend an extra day hiking to the site of Fossey's Karisoke Research Camp. The camp was established by Fossey on September 24, 1967 and remained operational until February 13, 1993 when during the Rwanda Civil War researchers abandoned the camp. Dr. Katie Fawcett, who was the Director of the DFGFI Karisoke Research Center from 2002-2011, tells the story of how not long after the camp was abandoned the Habyarimana government notified scientists who were working in the area that everything in the camp including many valuable scientific records had been either destroyed or stolen. Several months later she received a fax from the Rwandan Patriotic Front stating that everything had been taken to a safe place. The IMAX film *Mountain Gorilla* includes an interesting short sequence of the camp taken a couple of years prior to it being abandoned and destroyed.

Late in 1994 a new research center along with all the recovered equipment and scientific records from the original camp was established in the nearby town of Musanze where it remains operational today.

The trip to the site of the original Karisoke camp is well worth the time and effort. Here you can visit Fossey's gravesite located in the gorilla graveyard she established for her beloved Digit and other gorillas that died in the park while she was living at Karisoke. The original buildings were destroyed during the war, but foundations are still visible, including the ruins of the camp staff's barracks. To better appreciate the paradise-like setting of the camp, try to read Fossey's book *Gorillas in the Mist* before you go. And make sure you are prepared for what can be a strenuous muddy trek. Rubber boots, especially around the camp, are a must.

As you make the climb up "Fossey's mountain" to the top of the saddle between Mt. Visoke and Karisimbi, imagine all the hardworking porters who labored up the trail over the years. And try to imagine Dian Fossey walking up the trail with them. The people of the area called Fossey Nyiramachabelli (Kinyarwandan meaning "lone woman of the forest") and as you hike and gaze into the forest it's easy to sense her adventurous spirit.

The camp is surrounded by moss-laden Hagenia trees intermixed with all kinds of other gorilla foods including bamboo and several species of nettles. A few hours' hike to the southwest, across the border in the DRC, is Kabara Meadow. It was at Kabara that Carl Akeley, the founder of what was originally called Albert National Park, suddenly died and was buried on his last expedition to Africa in 1926. It was here also that George Schaller first studied mountain gorillas in 1959 and Dian Fossey began her studies in December 1966.

The research gorilla groups including Pablo's Group and Titus's Group all use this area of the park. You might find fresh gorilla droppings along the trail and come close to the gorillas themselves. Since the research groups are closely monitored, if they are near the trail when your group passes by, your guide will take you on a detour to prevent any kind of interaction. In order to maintain the scientific integrity of their observations, park visitors are normally not allowed near the research gorilla groups.

One of the most memorable moments of the hike is visiting the gravesite of Dian Fossey. In a clearing not far from the site of her cabin, Fossey is buried alongside the final resting places of some of her most beloved gorillas. You will want to take a moment to sit silently and remember her and the significance of her life as one of the world's most notable conservationists of all time.

Karisoke is surrounded by moss-laden Hagenia trees.

To sign up for the half-day hike arrangements need to be made in advance with RDB. Take a pair of binoculars in case you see some golden monkeys and birds along the way. It may be possible to take the hike on short notice if you have the energy and get back early from your gorilla trek. A permit is required, and as with all hikes into the Virungas you will be accompanied by a park guide and trackers.

Dian Fossey's gravesite at Karisoke with the inscription:

"NYIRAMACHABELLI"   DIAN FOSSEY 1932-1985   NO ONE LOVED GORILLAS MORE   REST IN PEACE, DEAR FRIEND   ETERNALLY PROTECTED IN THIS SACRED GROUND FOR YOU ARE HOME WHERE YOU BELONG

Golden Monkeys

Golden monkeys live in troops and spend most of their lives in trees. RDB has been leading tours to see the monkeys since 2001. Visitors who go on golden monkey treks need to be prepared for hiking in the park in the same way as they prepare for gorilla treks.

Trips leave from Kinigi park headquarters at 7:00am and last for two to three hours. You may also pre-arrange for trips to begin at other times. Once again, make sure that you bring a pair of binoculars and a telephoto lens to better observe and photograph these beautiful primates. Over 3,000 endangered golden monkeys inhabit Volcanoes National Park (see chapter 9). You can arrange for a morning visit by contacting RDB at Kigali, Musanze or at park headquarters at Kinigi.

Near headquarters behind the office you can visit the traditional site where the annual Gorilla Naming Ceremony is held. Every year during the month of June, thousands of people gather to celebrate the new baby gorillas born the previous year. Trackers and park staff come up with proposed names that are then selected by sponsors and honored guests.

Hiking to the top of the Volcanoes

If you are in shape and have the desire to hike to areas of the park that few people have ever seen, consider hiking to the tops of Mount Karisimbi, Mount Bisoke, or Mount Muhavura. Trips to the top of Karisimbi and Bisoke require a park guide and a permit from RDB. Access to Mount Muhavura is only from Mount Mgahinga National Park in Uganda where you will also need a permit. For more information on these dormant volcanic peaks see chapter three.

Musanze

In and around Musanze there are a number of places you can visit including a market, the RDB office, Hotel Muhabura, Lake Bulera and Lake Ruhondo. Ask your guide to include these locations on your itinerary since they are not easily found without a guide and high clearance vehicles.

Guide to Rwanda's Volcanoes National Park

Many guests enjoy a visit for lunch and/or spend the night at the Hotel Muhabura. Dian Fossey stayed at the Muhabura and there is a scene in the movie *Gorillas in the Mist* that looks like it could have been filmed there. Murals on the wall feature the Virunga Volcanoes and there is small gift shop in the reception area. Not everything sold in the shop is made in Rwanda so be sure to ask where the item comes from.

I grew to appreciate this hotel as my base in Rwanda when getting started on this book in 2005. Most of the staff speaks English and it's a good place to run into other tourists, park staff, Karisoke researchers, westerners working in Rwanda and locals who come by in the evening to watch soccer games and special gatherings in a large meeting room in the back. The hotel is the meeting place of the Musanze Lions Club and other groups. You might even run into Rwandan government officials and business men who often make the hotel restaurant a stopover when traveling the road between Kigali and Rubavu. The restaurant has a nice menu with Rwandan-French cuisine and at the bar you can try a variety of African beers. Ask about banana beer, a local favorite.

Topi are medium sized antelope often seen at Akagera National Park.

Akagera National Park

One of Rwanda's best kept secrets is Akagera National Park. The 347 square mile (900 square kilometers) park is made up of rolling hills, savanna grasslands, lakes and the Akagera River. The park borders the savannas of western Tanzania and is a popular spot for birdwatching and viewing large animals like hippos, antelope, elephant, crocodiles and more.

During the war the park suffered greatly from poaching, and wildlife numbers are not as great as they were during the 1980s. Fortunately the park is contiguous with the East African savanna of Tanzania's Ibanda and Rumanyika Game Reserves where many of the animals took refuge during the war and from which many are now returning. Like the rest of the country the park is on the upswing as the result of a government-private partnership that has helped to reestablish ecotourism. CNN reported a humorous story about how baboons and black-faced vervet monkeys had taken residence at the lodge during the war and refused to leave when the Akagera Game Lodge was reopened in 2004.

At this time you may not find the Big Five, but you won't leave disappointed either. The Acacia and Combretum woodlands, grasslands, swamps, lakes and Akagera River are home to pods of hippo, Cape eland, topi, impala, roan antelope, giraffe, zebra, buffalo, elephant and more. Over 500 bird species have been recorded in the park and plans are underway to reintroduce both lions and black rhinos. For those who like roughing it, Akagera offers camping opportunities on the shores of some of the lakes.

Like all ecotourism destinations in Rwanda visiting Akagera comes with an added bonus: the good feeling you will have knowing that your support as a visitor will help ensure the long-term protection of this beautiful natural area.

Nyungwe National Park

If you are coming to Africa to see primates you have come to the right place. Nyungwe (N-yoong-gway) National Park has 20% of all African primate species including chimpanzees, eastern needle-clawed galagos, greater bushbabies, black and white colobus monkeys, grey-cheeked mangabeys, L'Hoest's monkeys and rare owl-

Many people on primate safaris stop a Nyungwe National Park in hopes of seeing chimpanzees.

faced monkeys. The park is contiguous with the Kibira National Park in Burundi. Combined, these two protected areas form the largest block of forest in East and Central Africa.

To get the most of your visit take one to two days seeing the park and spend as much time hiking into the forest as time will allow. Like all wildlife habitats the more you head into the bush at different times of the day the more species you will see. The park's diversity of plant and animal life includes over 240 tree species, over 140 species of orchids and 275 species of birds. The Nyungwe Forest Conservation Project has published a little guide booklet to the park that is available from RDB offices and park headquarters.

Securing the Park's Future

The mountain gorillas of Volcanoes National Park are ambassadors for conservation. As this last chapter is written all is not well in the Virungas. Since 1996 war and conflict continues to impact nearby Virunga National Park where ten gorillas were killed in 2007. People around the world have followed the story in the news and on a blog hosted by virunga.org. As the conflict continues, Virunga National Park staff and researchers risk their lives and their families to to protect the gorillas and the Virunga ecosystem.

Silverbacks have no guns to protect themselves and their families. The gorillas have no one to represent them in courts of law. The babies and other little ones are totally helpless. These amazing creatures have always been and will always be unfortunate and innocent bystanders. Their future is in the hands of the people working and fighting to protect them. There is hope today only because there are people who care. If we ever let our guard down all could be lost forever.

The hard work and dedication required to protect Africa's crown jewel has not always come easy. Since 1994 over 140 park rangers have made the ultimate sacrifice with their lives, and sadly the struggle to protect the region is far from being won. Fortunately there are beacons of hope. They include people like Paulin Ngobobo, the Virunga National Park Senior Warden who has helped to report efforts at WildlifeDirect.org; Prince Emmanuel de Merode, Chief Warden of Virunga National Park who was seriously injured when he was shot during an ambush on April 15, 2014; and Felix Ndagijimana the first Rwanda appointed Director of the Karisoke Research Center; Let us remember them all in our thoughts and prayers.

Virunga National Park rangers were unable to adequately patrol the Gorilla Sector adjacent to Volcanoes National Park for over 14 months from 2007-2008 because of fighting between rebel forces and the Congolese Army. They were finally able to return in late November, 2008.

Young boy with the Virungas in the distance.

Securing the park's future

A secure future for Volcanoes National Park and the entire Virunga ecosystem is an important conservation goal for Rwanda and the world. Rwanda appears to be on the right track in recovering from the tragic events of 1994 and in developing a strong conservation program, but there is an incredible amount of progress to be made if the mountain gorillas and the park as an intact and secure ecosystem are to be achieved.

The home page of the International Gorilla Conservation Program at www.igcp.org is occasionally updated with a population estimate for the combined mountain gorilla population in the Virungas and Bwindi Impenetrable National Park. As of November 13, 2012 the combined population was estimated to be 880 gorillas. Both areas are seeing an increase in their respective gorilla populations. The most current mountain gorilla population census for the Virunga ecosystem was conducted in 2010 and found a significant increase in the size of the population compared to a census made in 2003. A count was made over a six-week period from March to April 2010 and estimated the population in the Virungas to be 480 individuals, up from 380 seven years earlier. A census conducted in Bwindi in 2012 estimated 400 mountain gorillas, up from 302 counted in 2006.

Of major concern to conservation efforts is the very large percentage of gorillas habituated to humans for both research (research groups) and ecotourism activities (tourist groups). The 2010 study found that over 50% of gorilla groups, which accounts for 73% of all gorillas, are habituated to the presence of humans. Over the past 35 years over two hundred thousand people have seen the habituated gorilla groups in Rwanda. Over time vulnerable gorilla groups become easy targets for poachers who look for opportunities to kill adult gorillas to sell their babies for the black market. Some gorillas, mainly outside of the Virungas region, are also killed for bushmeat. On an even more deplorable note the Congo massacre of July 2007 appears to indicate that some gorillas may also be killed for political reasons related to civil unrest and the illegal charcoal trade in the Eastern Congo.

In a press release issued within days of when four gorillas from the Rugendo Group in the DRC were massacred at Virungas National Park, the Director-General of UNESCO called upon the world to take notice:

The Director-General of UNESCO, Koïchiro Matsuura, is concerned over attacks perpetrated against the mountain gorillas of the Virunga National Park in the Democratic Republic of the Congo (DRC) and has called on the national authorities to adopt urgent measures to brings the killings to an end.

Declared a threatened species by the World Conservation Union (IUCN), the mountain gorilla is one of the Park's most important assets.

Situated in the north-east of the DRC, near the borders of Uganda and Rwanda, Virunga is known as the oldest African national park. Established in 1925, it was inscribed on the World Heritage List in 1979, for its natural habitats that are important for the preservation in situ of biological diversity, particularly some habitats in which survive threatened species of outstanding universal value from the scientific point of view or for conservation.

Securing the Park's Future

The four gorillas, one "silverback gorilla" and three females, slaughtered in Bukima, probably on the night of 22 July, belonged to a group inhabiting an area regularly visited by tourists. The disappearance of these gorillas represents not only a tragedy for the preservation of the species, but also the loss of an important source of revenue for local communities. Two other members of the group, a female and her young, are reported to have gone missing.

Since the beginning of the year, seven gorillas have been shot and killed. This is more than the numbers lost during the conflict that wracked the Great Lakes region in the 1990s, leading the World Heritage Committee to inscribe the park of the List of World Heritage in Danger.

The rising number of gorillas slaughtered in the southern part of Virunga National Park requires urgent measures to be taken.

The need for urgent measures to protect the gorillas and the park was also brought to the world's attention through the combined efforts of a broad coalition of conservation groups and media outlets including DFGFI, the World Wildlife Fund, the African Wildlife Foundation, WildlifeDirect.org, Newsweek Magazine, National Geographic, the BBC and the Discovery Channel. It is hoped that by informing larger numbers of people about what is happening in the Virungas the ecosystem can be saved.

A new emergency gorilla protection plan was launched within two weeks of the Congo massacre and by mid August, 2007 supplies to equip 150 new rangers were being flown in from Nairobi to help support a new permanent protection unit to watch over the gorilla groups in Virunga National Park. The gorilla rescue operation was directed by the DRC wildlife service called the Institut Congolais pour la Conservation de la Nature (ICCN) with the financial support and cooperation of WildlifeDirect, Zoological Society of London, Frankfurt Zoological Society, the International Gorilla Conservation Programme and DFGFI.

One year after the worst mountain gorilla massacre on record ICCN named Dr. Emmanuel de Merode as the new Director of Virunga National Park. Merode is the former CEO of WildlifeDirect. He assumed command of the park's 680 rangers on August 13, 2008 and less than one month later had already negotiated a troop withdrawal with the Congolese Army who had over 1000 soldiers deployed in the park. With the financial support of the European Union and Merode's new leadership, Congolese authorities hope to have a stronger hand in strengthening the rule of law,

In 2014 the UN had 21,189 troops in the Democratic Republic of Congo making it the largest peace keeping mission in the world.

stepping up antipoaching patrols and prevention of widespread forest destruction for charcoal. When this book was revised in June, 2014 conditions in Virunga National Park were stable and the park's website at virunga.org stated that the park was open and taking bookings for gorilla treks and accommodations at Mikeno Lodge, located at park headquarters at Rumangabo. The park was also planning treks to see the famous Nyiragango Volcano and the Tongo chimpanzees.

Virunga National Park Chief Warden Merode continues to help decrease tensions in the area where Mai Mai militias attacked the park and killed two rangers in 2012. The Africa Conservation Fund (UK) is currently managing the park with funds from the European Union. Over 3000 tourists a year are currently visiting the southern sector of the park. Currently the park has seven families of habituated gorillas, plus four solitary silverbacks for a total of 95 gorillas that tourists can come to see.

Park rangers in all three of the Virunga parks have tried to control illegal activities like poaching for many years. All of the good news from Rwanda in 2005 and 2006 was short-lived when over an eight year period sixteen baby mountain and Grauer's were rescued from poachers and from gorilla killing incidents in the DRC. As of June, 2014 twelve young Grauer's gorillas were being cared for at the Gorilla Rehabilitation and Conservation Education Center (GRACE) in the DRC (gracegorillas.org). At the Senkwekwe Center at Virunga National Park park headquarters, four young rescued mountain gorillas were being cared for by park staff (virunga.org/projects). A Scientific Technical Steering Committee involving all conservation partners in the region is helping to determine what happens to each gorilla. It is hoped that some, if not all, can successfully be released back into the wild.

In 2014 a new threat to Virunga National Park emerged from the British Petroleum Company Soco International. Soco was planning to explore for oil inside the park even though the park is protected by the DRC. According to the World Wildlife Fund oil development in the park would threaten local communities that depend on the park's natural resources. At Lake Edward for example more that 27,000 people fish for a living and over 50,000 people depend on the lake for their drinking water. A WWF online petition calls on people to help declare Virunga National Park off-limits to oil exploration because the park is far too valuable to be destroyed for short term financial gain.

Long term protection of the Virungas has been actively addressed by numerous organizations and government entities. There is little doubt that the development of a gorilla ecotourism industry has been a major incentive for all three third world governments controlling habitat conservation in the region. In Rwanda alone tourism is the country's highest source of foreign currency along with minerals, coffee and tea. Rwanda continues to show great progress in becoming a preferred African destination.

If the DRC can successfully turn things around and protect the gorillas and their habitat on their side of the border, long-term protection will be enhanced, but not guaranteed. There are other important threats to the Virungas, many of which were addressed by the first Intergovernmental Meeting on Great Apes and the first meeting of the Council of the Great Apes Survival Project (GRASP Council Meeting) convened in Kinshasa, DRC, in 2005. Anyone with an interest in more information about the conservation of mountain gorillas and other great apes should get a copy of the special GRASP report: World Atlas of Great Apes and their Conservation.

Threats to the park and the Virunga ecosystem include:

(1) Political instability in all three countries protecting the habitat.
(2) Socio-economic conditions outside the parks.
(3) Zoonotic diseases.
(4) Global warming.

Child soldiers in the Democratic Republic of Congo.

Political Instability in the Democratic Republic of Congo

No matter how well the Rwandan government protects Volcanoes National Park what happens in the DRC is critical to the Virunga ecosystem. No park is an island and there is little doubt that the gorillas and other creatures in the Virungas are threatened by human activities on any side of the border.

Thanks to those in the West who have supported conservation in Africa and the growing conservation movement on the continent, there is continued hope. But for hope to survive the larger issue of what is happening in the DRC must be addressed. An estimated 3.9 million people have died from war-related causes since the current conflict in the Democratic Republic of the Congo began in 2001. Nearly 80 percent of Congo's 56 million people live in extreme poverty and more than 70 percent are undernourished. The United Nations has its largest peacekeeping force in the world in the Congo, and in the summer of 2006, there was a glimmer of hope when the country held competitive national elections for the first time in more than 40 years.

As mountain gorillas were being massacred at Virungas National Park in 2007 the mineral-rich Eastern Congo experienced a widening escalation of political unrest. During the first seven months of that year over 230,000 people were forced from their homes to take refuge in displacement camps while U.N. officials warned that the area was on the brink of another all-out conflict. One rebel leader tried to take control of the region and called the area a new country "Land of the Volcanoes".

While all of this was going on at least 6,000 Rwandan Hutu militiamen were believed to be living in the area. Although many had assimilated themselves into Congo villages after a peace agreement was signed in 2004, they were never disarmed, and many remained organized under genocidal leaders. All of this reflects one simple reality: until the problem of the Rwandan Hutus and Tutsis is successfully addressed, the eastern Congo will remain a powder keg for many years to come.

United Nations Security Council.

The crisis is real. The crisis is complicated, but no matter how helpless you may feel in looking at the situation from a distance, there are ways you can help. One of the most significant actions you can take is to support non-profit organizations working on the ground in cooperation with the governments of the DRC and Rwanda. Important organizations you should learn about and support include these:

1. Dian Fossey Gorilla Fund International, www.gorillafund.org
2. Africa Conservation Fund, www.wildlifedirect.org
3. International Gorilla Conservation Program, www.igcp.org
4. Virunga National Park, www.virunga.org

If you live in the United States you can also call or write a letter to your representative in Congress and ask him or her to support increased federal dollars allocated to five separate funds dedicated to in-country conservation of great apes,

African elephants, Asian elephants, rhinos and tigers and marine turtles. The five Multinational Species Conservation Funds administered by the US Fish and Wildlife Service are authorized to receive $5 million apiece annually, yet Congress has never appropriated more than $1.4 million per year per program. There is public support for such an increase. For example, an online poll conducted by Newsweek Magazine in August of 2007 revealed that 65% of 13,396 respondents said that they would be willing to pay higher taxes in order to protect endangered species. Americans care about the world's wildlife and regularly show their support for conservation at zoos and aquariums that attract over 175 million visitors a year.

Socio-economic conditions outside the park

There are three important reasons why Rwanda has been successful in protecting Volcanoes National Park and the mountain gorillas: (1) an effective park staff consistently monitors habituated gorilla groups and other wildlife while making regular poaching patrols; (2) the government receives a great deal of support from non-profit organizations like the DFGFI, Mountain Gorilla Veterinary Project (MGVP) and IGCP; and (3) there is growing support for ecotourism from the Rwandan government and the local people living outside the park. RDB currently designates a percentage of park fees towards socio economic projects benefiting people in the surrounding communities. These designated funds are being used to target important projects that benefit large numbers of people including assistance with fresh water projects, schools and economic development.

A number of other international NGOs including many associated with zoos like the London and Frankfurt Zoological Societies are helping people make the connection between their well-being and the protection of the park. One organization that I have been involved with is the Partners in Conservation (PIC) project administered by the Columbus Zoo in Ohio. Since 1991 volunteers have raised funds to help protect wildlife like the mountain gorillas in the Virungas while working to help improve the lives of people living nearby. The conservation model used by PIC and government conservation agencies is well known in conservation circles around the world; respect the needs of the local people and they will help protect natural areas and wildlife.

Habituated mountain gorilla groups increasingly are seen searching for food outside the park in agricultural areas.

In addition to the need to develop more drinking water sources for people living near the park discussed earlier, there is also a tremendous need to provide the people in the surrounding communities with alternative sources of cooking fuel. Charcoal is a rare commodity everywhere and the illegal trade in charcoal production using trees growing in parks is having a major negative impact. Many people believe that the gorilla slaughter in 2007 was prompted by people heavily involved in this multi-million dollar industry.

Zoonotic diseases

Zoonotic diseases are human diseases acquired from or transmitted to any other vertebrate animal. Park staff and researchers routinely monitor the health of the gorillas and report any problems they encounter to field staff with the MGVP. The seriousness of potential gorilla health concerns was experienced in 1988 when a respiratory epidemic struck four of the seven habituated mountain gorilla groups and six gorillas died. Veterinarians suspected measles and nearly all the gorillas in the seven groups were vaccinated against the disease using blow darts.

Monitoring diseases and other health concerns such as parasites is a major part of DFGFI conservation efforts in partnership with MGVP and others. With the help of major corporations like Pfizer Pharmaceuticals, Inc., the DFGFI Ecosystem Health Program is helping prevent transmission of diseases between people and animals. Medicines have been donated and DFGFI has been able to help more than 200,000 people in Rwanda and Congo through ongoing parasite prevention and treatment programs.

Working in close cooperation with park rangers, guides and research staff, MGVP field veterinarians routinely visit habituated gorilla groups to look for health problems. Animals are treated for conditions that can affect their overall well-being in much the same way that a veterinarian watches over domestic animals. Physical contact is kept to a minimum and only when there are life-threatening problems such as a snare wrapped around a limb or some other life threatening injury is an animal anesthetized. With the exception of taking in an infant that has been orphaned, all contact is made in the wild and in close cooperation with park staff that are needed to help keep other gorillas in the group away from the rescue operation. You can follow the work of MGVP in the Virungas on their blog at www.gorilladoctorsblog.org. MGVP is one of the few conservation efforts providing health care for endangered species in the wild.

Nature oftentimes is allowed to take its course, especially when gorillas have health problems that are caused by other gorillas. For example, Nyakalima, a lone silverback who followed the Sabyinyo Group from 2005-8 had a severe injury to his right eye that was believed to have resulted from a fight with the silverback Guhonda. MGVP staff determined that any treatment to the injured eye could endanger the other eye and potentially cause blindness. Up until he died in 2008, Nyakalima appeared to have thrived with one eye. If he had outlived Guhonda, he could have taken over the entire group.

Global warming

Scientists are now making projections on how global warming might affect equatorial rainforests in Africa. A British and Uganda Scientist report in 2006 concluded that the glaciers in the Rwenzori Mountains, part of the Albertine Rift and home to one of four of the world's remaining tropical ice fields, are projected to disappear within two decades because of global warming. So far they have not seen any measurable changes in rainfall, but rising temperatures could affect agriculture and expand the range of tropical diseases.

The biodiversity of the Virungas is threatened by global warming largely because of how warmer temperatures reduce the size of habitats for plants and animals adapted to the cold. As temperatures warm, plants adapted to warmer temperatures will invade an area and significantly alter the plant diversity that many animals like mountain gorillas need to survive.

Conservation Education

People around the world need to understand why the future of humanity is directly connected to the protection of the environment, not just where they live, but also at faraway places like Volcanoes National Park. The mountain gorillas are helping to maintain an important ecosystem that is providing numerous benefits to people today and a long list of potential benefits in the future. You and I may understand this, but if the people who live near the park and in the region do not, the gorillas and the Virungas have a very uncertain future. That is why ecotourism and educational efforts like those sponsored by the DFGFI Karisoke Research Center are so important.

Gorillas, like other large animals at the top of the rainforest food pyramid, are valuable in helping to maintain the complex biodiversity where they live. Their foraging behavior helps to disperse seeds of numerous plants important to their own survival and the survival of countless other species. Few scientists will argue the belief that all species have some value even if they are not fully understood. In his writings for the U.S. Fish and Wildlife Service Endangered Species Bulletin, Jim Lyzer helps to bring this important understanding into focus:

Securing the Park's Future

"We are destroying or wiping out species before we know what their value might be. That in itself should justify the time and expense that it takes to help them avert extinction. Beyond that we have an ethical obligation to all the species that share this planet. When we lose anything, we're really losing a figurative encyclopedia. And we might be losing a page with enormous benefits to mankind. Unfortunately, today most people around the world either are unaware or unconcerned about the consequences that will surely affect the survival of our own species in the near future."

Now you know more about Volcanoes National Park than you probably ever thought to ask. You may also have many more questions than were answered in this book. If that's case I am glad, because the more that people think about Rwanda, the more people will hopefully get involved in helping the country move forward.

If you are planning a trip in the near future or are already there, I hope that you will spend the time to really get to know and understand Volcanoes National Park. I also hope that seeing the mountain gorillas and all the park has to offer will inspire you to do more than come to the park as a visitor. That's what happened to me and was the main reason why I wrote this little guide book.

Make a place in your heart for the Virungas to live forever. If you do, chances are good that you will want to join others in helping to preserve this international treasure for all time.

If you are never able to make the journey in person, I hope that you will make the journey in your mind. Appreciate the wonders of the world and know that you too are part of it. The fate of the gorillas and the Virungas is the fate of humankind. Their survival is our survival. If the world cannot be made safe for them, it will certainly not be a very safe place for people.

Bibliography

*Highly recommended by the author

Africa-America Institute. *U.S. Tour to Highlight Rwanda's Bold Approach in Fighting Poverty Using New Technologies.* October 25, 2005.

Africa. Encyclopedia Britannica. *Encyclopedia Britannica 2007 Deluxe Edition.* Chicago: Encyclopedia Britannica, 2007.

Africa Museum. *Papilio antimachus* DRURY, www.africamuseum.be, Accessed July 20, 2007.

African Wildlife Foundation. *Conservation of Afro-Montane Forest and Mountain Gorillas in a Landscape Context*, 2005.

Alden, Estes, Schlitter and McBride. National Audubon Society Field Guide to African Wildlife. Alfred A. Knopf, 1995.

American Geophysical Union University College Press Release. Fabled Equatorial African Icecaps to Disappear. May 15, 2006.

*Animal Planet. *Saving a Species: Gorillas on the Brink.* DVD, 2008.

Areste, Manual and Rafael Cebrian. *Snakes of the World.* Sterling Publishing Company, 2003.

Associated Press Report. Rwanda game lodge reopens to human guests. CNN.com Travel Section, February 10, 2004.

BarackObama.com, June 9, 2007.

*Bedoyere, Camilla de la. *No One Loved Gorillas More, Dian Fossey Letters from the Mist.* National Geographic, 2005.

Beringe, R. von Bericht des Hauptmanns von Beringe Aber seine Expedition nach

BIBLIOGRAPHY

Ruanda. Deutsches Kolonialblatt, 1903.

Beston, Henry A. *The Outermost House.* Doubleday and Doran, 1928.

Campbell, Bob. *The Taming of the Gorillas.* Minerva Press LTD, 2000.

Carr, Rosamond. *American in Rwanda.* National Public Radio, July 28, 2003.

Chaveas, Mike, Gritzner, Jason and Gurrieri, Joe. USDA Forest Service Technical Assistance Trip. *Virunga – Bwindi Region: Republic of Rwanda, Republic of Uganda, Democratic Republic of Congo.* March 4 – 21, 2005.

Chidester, Judy A. *Getting to know a gorilla...Charlie was a girl and real cuddly.* Department of State Newsletter, April, 1980.

Childs, Simon. Rehabilitating Eastern Gorillas. Gorilla Journal 34, June, 2007.

Clinton, William J, *My Life.* Random House, 2004.

Cousins, Don and Huffman, Michael A. *Medicinal Properties in the Diet of Gorillas: An Ethno-Pharmacological Evaluation,* African Study Monographs, 23(2): 65-89. 2002.

D. Brann Union Institute. *Abstract of the 24th Annual Meeting of the American Society of Primatologists,* August, 2001.

Debonnet, Guy. UNESCO, Personal Communication, July 4, 2005.

Dian Fossey Gorilla Fund International. Gorilla Staple Food Database (unpublished). 2007.

Dian Fossey Gorilla Fund International. *Virunga Volcanoes Range Mountain Gorilla Census,* 2003 (unpublished manuscript).

Dian Fossey Gorilla Fund International Field News. Dian Fossey Gorilla Fund International, October, 2004.

Dian Fossey Gorilla Fund International, Field News. Dian Fossey Gorilla Fund International, January, 2000.

Dian Fossey Gorilla Fund International Plant and Animal Database (unpublished), 2005, 2007.

Dian Fossey Gorilla Fund Endemic Plant Species Database (unpublished), 2007.

Dian Fossey Gorilla Fund International, Karisoke Research Center. *The Volcanoes National Park Training Manual: Primates.* (unpublished) 2005.

Dian Fossey Gorilla Fund International, Karisoke Research Center PowerPoint Report. The Golden Monkey, Ecology, and Behavior (unpublished), 2005.

Encyclopedia Britannica. *Pleistocene Epoch.* Encyclopedia Britannica 2007 Deluxe Edition.

Chicago: Encyclopedia Britannica.

Encyclopedia Britannica. *Kagera River.* Encyclopedia Britannica 2007 Deluxe Edition.

Chicago: Encyclopedia Britannica.

Encyclopedia Britannica. *White-toothed shrew* (genus *Crocidura*). Encyclopedia Britannica 2007 Deluxe Edition. Chicago: Encyclopedia Britannica.

Fawcett, Katie. Karisoke Research Center, Personal Communication, June 15, 2005.

Fawcett, Katie. Karisoke Research Center, Personal Communication, September 19, 2005.

*Fossey, Dian. *Gorillas in the Mist.* The University of Chicago Press, 1981.

Freedom of Information Request to Georgianne Nienaber, 2006. Relayed to the author from Dr. Shirley McGreal, International Primate Protection League, May 18, 2007.

Furniss, Charlie. The Wonder Plant with an Uncertain Future. Geographical, August, 2004.

Furniss, Charles. *Protected Areas.* Geographical, June, 2005.

Gorilla Journal. June, 2002.

Gorilla Sanctuary. Time Magazine, October, 22, 1928.

Great Ape Survival Bulletin. Volume 113, No. 1, September 12, 2005.

Grzimek's Animal Life Encyclopedia, Birds I. Van Nostrand Reinhold, 1972.

BIBLIOGRAPHY

Guber-Peters Company. *Gorillas in the Mist, the Story of Dian Fossey, 1988.*

*Halsey Carr, Rosamond. *Land of a Thousand Hills.* Viking Penguin, 1999.

International Gorilla Conservation Program et al. Unpublished Report. Virunga Volcanoes Range, Mountain gorilla census, 2005.

*International Union for the Conservation of Nature. *World Atlas of Great Apes and their Conservation,* 2005.

International Union for the Conservation of Nature. Redlist.org. Accessed June 1, 2007.

Kalina, J. *Mgahinga Gorilla National Park: Reference for Management.* Berichdas Ministry of Tourism and Wildlife, Kampala, Uganda, 1993.

Kalinijabo, John. Personal Communication. June 20, 2007.

*Kinzer, Stephen, A Thousand Hills, (John Wiley and Sons, 2008).

Kohler, Marcus. Rwanda's Forests and Mountains. Naturetrek Tour Report, pp. 10- 24 September, 2005.

Last Refuge, LTD. *The Gorillas of My Grandfather*, DVD, 2004.

Layzer, Jim. Sending surrogates to the rescue. Endangered Species Bulletin March/April, 2003.

Lejju, J. B., Oryem-Origa, H. and Kasese, J. M. East African Wild Life Society, *African Journal of Ecology*, 39, 65-73, 2001.

Lilly, Alecia. Dian Fossey Gorilla Fund International, Personal Communication, 2007.

Loven, Jennifer. *Rwanda hopeful, Laura Bush says.* Associated Press, July 15, 2005.

McCrummen, Stephanie. For Tutsis of Eastern Congo, Protector, Exploiter or Both? Washington Post Foreign Service. pp A01. August 6, 2007.

National Geographic. *The Lost Film of Dian Fossey.* 2002.

Neinaber, Georgianne. *An Interview with Rosamond Carr.* International Primate Protection League, Dec. 21, 2005.

Nowak, Ronald M. *Walker's Mammals of the World* Fifth Edition, Volume I and II, The John Hopkins University Press, 1991.

Nzabonimana, Oliver. Personal Communication, February 19 and June 3 and 18, 2007.

McGrew ET. et al. *Great Ape Societies.* Cambridge University Press, 1996.

MD Travel Health. www.mdtravelhealth.com, Accessed July 24, 2007.

Miller, Scott E. Lucie M. Rogo. Challenges and opportunities in understanding and utilization of African insect diversity Cimbebasia 17: pp. 197-218, 2001.

Minja, M. M. J. The Maasai Wonder Plants. *Paper presented at the People and Plants training workshop*, Tropical Pesticides Training Institute, Arusha, Tanzania, 1999.

Mittermeir, Russell A. et al. *Hotspots Revisited: Earth's Biologically Richest and Most Endangered Terrestrial Ecoregions.* CEMEX, 2004.

*Mountain Gorilla and Company. *IMAX Mountain Gorilla*, DVD, 1991.

Mowat, Farley. *Woman in the Mists: The Story of Dian Fossey and the Mountain Gorillas of Africa.* Warner Books Inc. 1987.

Munyaneza, James and Bigabo, Patrick. *Clinton again regrets failure to stop Genocide.* The New Times. July 24, 2005.

Oliver, William L. R. Status Survey and Conservation Action Plan: Pigs, Peccaries, and Hippos, Chapter 4. IUCN, 1993.

Owiunji, I et al. *Biological Survey of Virunga Volcanoes*, Wildlife Conservation Society et al. 2005.

Plumptre A. J. et al. The Biodiversity of the Albertine Rift, Albertine Rift Technical Report Series, Number 3, Wildlife Conservation Society, 2003.

Plumptre, A. J., McNeilage, A., Hall, J. S. and Williamson, E. A. *The current status of gorillas and threats to their existence at the beginning of the new millennium.* In: *Gorilla Biology, A Multidisciplinary Perspective* (Taylor and Goldsmith, editors). Cambridge University Press, 2003.

BIBLIOGRAPHY

Republic of Rwanda, Ministry Lands, Resettlement and Environment. National Strategy and Action Plan for the Conservation of Biodiversity in Rwanda, 2003.

Rwanda Gateway www.rwandagateway.org, Accessed July 21, 2007.

Salopek, Paul F. *The Mountain Gorillas of Africa*. National Geographic, October, 1995.

Schaller, G. B. *The Conservation of Gorillas in the Virunga Volcanoes*. Current Anthropology, I (4), 1960.

Schaller, George B. *Gorilla: Struggle for Survival in the Virungas*. Aperture Foundation, 1962.

Schaller, George B. *The Mountain Gorilla: Ecology and Behavior*. University of Chicago Press, 1963.

Schaller, George B. The *Year of the Gorilla*. The University of Chicago Press, 1964.

*Schaller, George and Michael Nichols. Gorilla Struggle for Survival in the Virungas. Aperture Books, 1989.

Sholley, Craig. Guerillas in the Midst of Gorillas. www.irwc-online.org, Accessed August 2, 2007

Steklis, Gerald N. and Steklis, H.D. *The value of long-term research: The mountain gorilla as a case study*. In: Stoinski, T., Steklis, H.D. and Mehlman, P.T. (eds.) pp. 150-173,

Conservation in the 21st Century: Gorillas as a Case Study. New York, NY: Springer, 2007.

Stevenson, Terry and John Fanshawe. The Birds of East Africa: Kenya, Tanzania, Uganda, Rwanda, Burundi. Princeton Field Guides, 2001.

Stoinski, Tara. Field News, Dian Fossey Gorilla Fund International, March, 2006.

Stoinski, Tara. Personal Communication, Dian Fossey Gorilla Fund International, February, 2007.

The Inaugural Kirkpatrick National Lecture featuring: President Paul Kagame, *The Norman Transcript*, April 27, 2006.

U.S. Department of State. *International Religious Freedom Report*, released by the Bureau of Democracy, Human Rights and Labor, November 8, 2005.

UNESCO, *Mgahinga Gorilla National Park*. www.whc.unesco.org, Accessed June 30, 2007.

UNESCO. Director-General voices concern over fate of Virunga National Park gorillas. Press Release, August 3, 2007.

*Weber, Bill, and Amy Vedder. *In the Kingdom of Gorillas: Fragile Species in a Dangerous Land*, Touchstone Books, 2002.

Wildlife Conservation Society. *Albertine Rift Programme*, 2005.

Wildlife Conservation Society. www.wcs.org. *International Conservation, Africa Program. Accessed* June 25, 2007.

Wildlife Conservation Society. Akagera National Park. From www.wcs.org, Accessed June 1, 2007.

Wilson, Vivian J. *The Duikers of Africa*. Directory Publishers Limited, 2001.

World Wildlife Fund. Rare Okapi Sighted in Eastern Congo Park. Press Release, June 8, 2006.

Appendix

Gorilla Conservation Organizations

In addition to the Dian Fossey Gorilla Fund International, Wildlife Direct, Virunga Alliance and Berggorilla & Regenwald Direkthilfe Gorilla Journal mentioned in chapter 5, the author also recommends that you look into supporting the Frankfurt Zoological Society, International Gorilla Conservation Program, Mountain Gorilla Veterinarian Project, Wildlife Conservation Society and Zoological Society of London. Links to other related groups associated with the United Nation's Great Apes Survival Project (GRASP) can be found on the GRASP Partner page at www.unep.org/grasp under NGOs and Other Supporting Partners. A number of accredited Zoos in the United States are also active in gorilla conservation projects including the Wildlife Conservation Society at the Bronx Zoo. To learn more about Zoos involved with gorilla conservation projects visit their websites at www.aza.org.

Dian Fossey Gorilla Fund International
www.gorillafund.org

Wildlife Direct
www.wildlifedirect.org

The Gorilla Organization
www.gorillas.org

Berggorilla & Regenwald Direkthilfe Gorilla Journal
www.berggorilla.de

Frankfurt Zoological Society
www.zoo-frankfurt.de

International Gorilla Conservation Program
www.igcp.org

Mountain Gorilla Veterinarian Project
www.mgvp.org

Volcanoes National Park
www.rwandatourism.com

Virunga National Park (Virunga Alliance)
www.virunga.org

Wildlife Conservation Society
www.wcs.org

Zoological Society of London
www.zsl.org

Gorillas Nest Lodge.

Tour Operators in Rwanda

There are many tour operators who can help you plan a trip to the park. The best place to begin is by looking at the Travel Guide at www.rwandatourism.com.

For further information contact:
Rwanda Development Board (Formerly ORTPN) P.O. Box 6239 KIGALI, RWANDA.
Telephone (+250) 252573396 or (+250) 2522502350.
Email: reservation@rwandatourism.com

Volcanoes National Park Bird List

Data Compiled by the Karisoke Research Institute.

Species   **Status**

Family Podicipedidae
Little Grebe, *Tachybaptus ruficollis*   Uncommon

Family Ardeidae (Heron, night-heron, egret, bittern)
Black-Headed Heron, *Ardea melanocephala*   Uncommon
Cattle Egret, *Bubulcus ibis*   Uncommon

Family Scopidae (Hammerhead)
Hammerkop, *Scopus umbretta*   Uncommon

Family Ciconiidae (Storks)
Abdim's Stork, *Ciconia abdimii*   Uncommon
White Stork, *Ciconia ciconia*   Rare

Family Threskiornithidae
Hadada ibis, *Bostrychia hagedash*   Uncommon

Family Anatidae (Waterfowl)
Egyptian Goose, *Alopochen aegyptiacus*   Uncommon
Hottentot Teal, *Anas Hottentota*   Uncommon
Garganey Teal, *Anas querquedula*   Uncommon
African Black Duck, *Anas sparsa*   Uncommon
Yellow-Billed Duck, *Anas undulata*   Uncommon
Maccoa Duck, *Oxyura maccoa*   Uncommon

Bird List

Family Accipitridae (Vultures and Eagles)

Rufous-Breasted Sparrow hawk, *Accipiter rufiventris*	Rare
Black Sparrow hawk, *Accipiter melanoleucus*	Uncommon
African Goshawk, *Accipiter tachiro*	Uncommon
Tawny Eagle, *Aquila rapax*	Uncommon
Wahlberg's Eagle, *Aquila wahlbergi*	Uncommon
Crowned Hawk Eagle, *Polemaetus/ Stephanoaetus coronatus*	Uncommon
Harrier Hawk, *Polyboroides radiatus*	Uncommon
Augur Buzzard, *Buteo rufofuscus*	Uncommon
Common Buzzard / Eurasian Buzzard, *Buteo buteo*	Common
Mountain Buzzard, *Buteo oroephilus*	Common
Black-shouldered Kite, *Elanus caeruleus*	Common
Long-crested Eagle, *Lophaetus occipitalis*	Uncommon
Bat Hawk, *Macheiramphus alcinus*	Uncommon
Black Kite, *Milvus migrans*	Uncommon
European Honey-Buzzard, *Pernis apivorus*	Uncommon
Martial Eagle, *Polemaetus bellicosus*	Uncommon
African Crowned Eagle, *Stephanoaetus coronatus*	Uncommon
African Harrier-Hawk or Gymnogene, *Polyboroides typus*	Uncommon
Bateleur Eagle, *Terathopius ecaudatus*	Uncommon
White-Headed Vulture, *Trigonoceps occipitalis*	Uncommon

Family Falconidae (Falcons)

Lanner Falcon, *Falco biarmicus*	Uncommon
African Hobby, *Falco cuvierii*	Rare
Peregrine Falcon, *Falco peregrinus*	Uncommon
Eurasian Hobby, *Falco subbuteo*	Uncommon
Eurasian Kestrel, *Falco tinnunculus*	Uncommon
Lesser Kestrel, *Falco naumanni*	

Family Pandionidae (Ospreys)

Osprey, *Pandion haliaetus*	Rare

Family Phasianidae
European Quail / Common Quail	Uncommon
Red-necked Spurfowl, *Francolin afer*	Uncommon
Handsome francolin, *Francolinus nobilis*	Common
Red-winged francolin, *Francolinus levaillantii*	Uncommon

Family Gruidae (Cranes)
Sudan Crowned Crane, *Balearica pavonina*	Uncommon
Gray Crowned-Crane, *Balearica regulorum*	Rare

Family Rallidae (Rails, Coots, Moorhens, Gallinules)
Red-knobbed Coot, *Fulica cristata*	Uncommon
Buff-Spotted Crake, *Sarothrura elegans*	Uncommon

Family Charadriidae (Plovers, Lapwings)
Caspian Plover, *Charadrius asiaticus*	Uncommon

Family Scolopacidae (Sandpipers)
Common Snipe, *Gallinago gallinago*	Uncommon
Common Sandpiper, *Actitis hypoleucos*	Uncommon
European Snipe, *Capella gallinago*	Uncommon
African Snipe, *Gallinago nigripennis*	Uncommon
Curlew, *Numenins arguata*	Uncommon
Common Sandpiper, *Tringa hypoleucos*	Uncommon
Wood Sandpiper, *Tringa glareola*	Uncommon
Green Sandpiper, *Tringa ochropus*	Uncommon

Family Columbidae (Doves, Pigeons)
Rameron Pigeon / Olive Pigeon, *Columba arquatrix*	Common
Speckled Pigeon, *Columba guinea*	Uncommon

Bird List

Dusky Turtle-Dove, *Streptopelia lugens*	Uncommon
Tambourine Dove, *Turtur tympanistria*	Common
Red-Eyed Dove, *Streptopelia semitorquata*	Uncommon

Family Psittacidae

Brown-Necked Parrot. *Poicephalus robustus*	Uncommon

Family Musophagidae

Ruwenzoni Turaco, *Tauraco /Ruwenzorornis johnstoni*	Common

Family Cuculidae

Blue-Headed Coucal, *Centropus monachus*	Uncommon
White-Browed Coucal, *Centropus superciliosus*	Uncommon
Yellowbill, *Ceuthmochares aereus*	Uncommon
Klaas's Cuckoo, *Chrysococcyx klaas*	Uncommon
Levallant's Cuckoo, *Clamator levaillantii*	Uncommon
European Cuckoo or Common Cuckoo, *Cuculus canorus*	Uncommon
Lesser Cuckoo/ Madagascar Cuckoo, *Cuculus poliocephalus / rochii*	Uncommon

Family Estrildidae

Bronze Munia, *Lonchura cucullata*	Rare

Family Tytonidae (Owls)

African / Abyssinian long-eared owl, *Asio abyssinicus*	Uncommon
Marsh Owl, *Asio capensis*	Uncommon
Spotted Eagle Owl, *Bubo africanus*	Uncommon
African Wood Owl, *Ciccaba woodfordii*	Uncommon
Cape Grass Owl / African Grass Owl, *Tyto capensis*	Uncommon
African Wood Owl, *Strix woodfordii*	Uncommon

Zosteropidae

African Yellow White-Eye, *Zosterops senegalensis*	Common

Family Caprimulgidae
Montane Nightjar, *Caprimulgus ruwenzorii* — Common
Pennant-Winged Nightjar, *Macrodipteryx vexillarius* — Uncommon

Family Apodidae (Swifts)
Mottled Swift, *Apus / Tachymarptis aequatorialis* — Common
European Swift / Common Swift
Alpine Swift, *Apus apus* — Uncommon
Scarce Swift, *Apus / Tachymarptis melba* — Uncommon

Family Coliidae
Speckled Mousebird, *Colius striatus* — Common

Family Meropidae (Bee-eaters)
European Bee-Eater, *Merops apiaster* — Common
Cinnamon-chested Bee-Eater, *Merops oreobates* — Uncommon

Family Coraciidae (Kingfishers and Rollers)
Lilac-Breasted Roller, *Coracias caudata* — Rare
Broad-Billed Roller, *Eurystomus glaucurus* — Rare

Family Phoeniculidae (Woodhoopoes)
White-Headed Wood-Hoopoe, *Phoeniculus bollei* — Uncommon

Family Bucerotidae (Hornbills)
Crowned Hornbill, *Tockus alboterminatus* — Common

Family Capitonidae (Barbets)
Western Tinkerbird, *Pogoniulus coryphaeus* — Uncommon
Yellow-Rumped Tinkerbird, *Pogoniulus bilineatus* — Common

Bird List

Family Picidae (Woodpeckers)
Fine-Banded Woodpecker, *Campethera tullbergi*	Uncommon
Cardinal Woodpecker, *Dendropicos fuscescens*	Uncommon
Olive Woodpecker, *Dendropicos Mesopicos/griseocephalus*	Common

Family Alaudidae (Larks)
Rufous-Naped Lark, *Mirafra africana*	Uncommon

Family Hirundinidae (Swallows)
Black Saw-wing, *Psalidoprocne holomelas*	Common
European House Martin / Common House Martin, *Delichon urbica*	Uncommon
European Swallow / Barn Swallow, *Hirundo rustica*	Uncommon
African Sandmartin / Plain Martin, *Riparia paludicola*	Common
European Sandmartin / Bank Swallow, *Riparia riparia*	Uncommon

Family Motacillidae (Wagtail, Pipit)
Richard's Pipit, *Anthus anthus*	Common
African Pied Wagtail, *Monticilla aguimp*	Uncommon
Yellow Wagtail, *Monticilla flava*	Uncommon

Family Campephagidae (Cuckoo-shrikes, Trillers)
Grey Cuckoo-Shrike, *Coracina caesia*	Uncommon

Family Laniidae (Shrikes)
Black Cuckoo-Shrike, *Campephaga sulphurata / flava*	Rare
Northern Puffback, *Dryoscopus gambensis*	Uncommon
Mountain Sooty Shrike (Boubou), *Dryoscopus gambensis*	Uncommon
Fiscal Shrike/ Common fiscal, *Laniarius poensis*	Uncommon
Mackinnon's Grey Shrike, *Lanius collaris*	Common
Donherty's BushShrike, *Lanius mackinnoni*	Common
Lagden's BushShrike, *Malaconotus dohertyi*	Common

Family Turdidae (Thrushes)

White-Browed Robin-Chat, *Cossypha heuglini*	Uncommon
Cape Robin Chat, *Cossypha caffra*	Common
Archer's Robin-Chat, *Dessonornis archeri*	Common
Stone Chat / African Stonechat, *Saxicola torquata*	Common
Olive Thrush, *Turdus olivaceus*	Common
African Thrush, *Turdus pelios*	Rare
Abyssinian Ground-Thrush, *Zoothera piaggiae*	Uncommon
Kivu Ground-Thrush, *Zoothera tanganjicae*	Common
White-Starred Bush Robin, *Pogonocichla stellata*	Common

Family Timaliidae (Whipbirds, Babblers)

Mountain Illadopsis, *Illadopsis pyrrhoptera*	Uncommon
Abyssinian Hill Babbler, *Alcippe/ Pseudoalcippe abyssinica*	Common
Black-Lored Babbler, *Turdoides sharpei*	Uncommon

Family Sylviidae (Warblers, Babblers)

White-browed Crombec, *Sylvietta leucophrys*	Uncommon
Masked Apalis, *Apalis binotata*	Uncommon
Chestnut-Throated Apalis, *Apalis porphyrolaema*	Common
Collared Apalis, *Apalis ruwenzorii*	Uncommon
Cinnamon Bracken-Warbler, *Bradypterus cinnamomeus*	Uncommon
Grauer's Rush Warbler, *Bradypterus graueri*	Uncommon
Wing-Snapping Cisticola, *Cisticola ayersii*	Common
Chubb's Cisticola, *Cisticola chubbi*	Common
Red-Faced Woodland-Warbler, *Phylloscopus laetus*	Common
Willow Warbler, *Phylloscopus trochilus*	Common
Brown Woodland-Warbler, *Phylloscopus umbrovirens*	Common
Banded Prinia, *Prinia bairdii*	Uncommon
Tawny-Flanked Prinia, *Prinia subflava*	Uncommon
Blackcap, *Sylvia atricapilla*	Uncommon
Garden Warbler, *Sylvia borin*	Uncommon

Bird List

Family Muscicapidae (Flycatcher)
White-Eyed Slaty Flycatcher, *Melaenornis fischeri*	Common
Pied Flycatcher, *Ficedula hypoleuca*	Common
Ruwenzori Puff-Backed Flycatcher/ Ruwe, *Batis diops*	Uncommon
Chin-Spot Puff-Backed Flycatcher/ Chinspot, *Batis molitor*	Common
Mountain Yellow Flycatcher, *Chloropeta similis*	Common
White-Eyed Slaty Flycatcher, *Melaenornis fischeri*	Common
African Dusky Flycatcher, *Muscicapa adusta=Alseonax*	Rare
Collared Flycatcher, *Muscicapa albicollis=Ficedula*	Uncommon
Paradise Flycatcher, *Phyllomyias griseiceps*	Common
White-Tailed Crested Flycatcher, *Trochocercus albonotatus*	Uncommon

Family Paridae (Chickadees, Titmouse)
Stripe-Breasted Tit, *Parus fasciiventer*	Common

Family Pycnonotidae (Bulbuls, Greenbuls)
Yellow-Whiskered Greenbul (Bulbul), *Andropadus latirostris*	Common
Olive-Breasted Mountain Greenbul, *Andropadus tephrolaema*	Uncommon
Common Bulbul, *Pycnonotus barbatus*	Common

Family Nectariniidae (Sunbirds)
Blue-Headed Sunbird, *Cinnyris / Cyanomitra alinae*	Uncommon
Northern-Double Collared Sunbird, *Cinnyris preussi*	Uncommon
Regal Sunbird, *Cinnyris regia*	Common
Rwenzori Double-collared Sunbird, *Cinnyris stuhlmanni*	Common
Variable Sunbird, *Cinnyris venusta*	Common
Malachite Sunbird, *Nectarinia famosa*	Uncommon
Scarlet-Tufted Malachite Sunbird, *Nectarinia johnstoni*	Common
Bronze-Sunbird, *Nectarinia kilimensis*	Uncommon
Northern-Double-Collared Sunbird, *Nectarinia/Cynnyris preussi*	Common
Purple-Breasted Sunbird, *Nectarinia purpureiventris*	Uncommon

Family Fringillidae (Goldfinches, Crossbills)

Thick-Billed Seed-Eater, *Serinus burtoni*	Uncommon
African Citril, *Serinus citrinelloides*	Common
Yellow-Crowned Canary / Cape Canary, *Serinus canicollis*	Common
Streaky Seed-Eater, *Serinus striolatus*	Common
Brimstone Canary, *Serinus sulphuratus*	Common

Family Estrildidae (Waxbills)

Common Waxbill, *Estrilda astrild*	Rare
Black-Headed Waxbill, *Estrilda atricapilla*	Common
Black-Crowned Waxbill, *Estrilda nonnula*	Common
Yellow-Bellied Waxbill, *Estrilda quartinia*	Common
Shelley's Crimson-wing, *Cryptospiza shelleyi*	Uncommon
Dusky Crimson-wing, *Cryptospiza jacksoni*	Uncommon

Family Emberizidae (Sparrows, Grosbeaks, Longspurs)

Sooty Chat, *Myrmecocichla nigra*	Common
Grey-Headed Sparrow, *Passer griseus*	Rare

Family Ploceidae (Sparrows, Weavers, Bishops)

Yellow Bishop, *Euplectes capensis*	Uncommon
Strange Weaver, *Ploceus alienus*	Common
Stuhlmann's Baglafecht Weaver, *Ploceus baglafecht*	Common

Family Sturnidae (Starlings and Mynas)

Yellow-Billed Oxpecker, *Buphagus africanus*	Common
Slender-Billed Chestnut-Winged Starling, *Onychognatus tenuirostris*	Uncommon

Family Corvidae (Crows, magpies, jays, nutcrackers)

Pied Crow, *Corvus albus*	Common
White-Necked Raven, *Corvus albicollis*	Common

Volcanoes National Park Mammal List

Data Compiled by the Karisoke Research Institute

Family Chrysochloridae
Golden Mole, *Chlortalpa leucorhina*
Stuhlmann's Golden Mole, *Chrysochloris stuhlmanni*

Family Soricidae (Shrews)
Long-Tailed Musk Shrew, *Crocidura dolichura*
Northern Swamp Musk Shrew, *Crocidura maurisca*
Kivu Shrew, *Crocidura kivuana*
Long-Haired Kivu Shrew, *Crocidura lanosa*
Butiaba Musk Shrew, *Crocidura littoralis*
Matschie's Musk Shrew, *Crocidura nigrofusca*
Rwenzori Musk Shrew, *Crocidura niobe*
Musk Shrew, *Crocidura occidentalis*
Northern Giant Musk Shrew, *Crocidura olivieri*
Hero Shrew, *Scutisorex somereni*
Forest Musk Shrew, *Suncus ruandae*
Least Long-Tailed Forest Shrew, *Sylvisorex granti*
Forest Shrew, *Sylvisorex lunarias*
Forest Shrew, *Sylvisorex volcanorum*

Family Tenrecidae
Rwenzori Otter Shrew, *Micropotamogale ruwenzorii*

Family Pteropopidae
Rousette Fruit Bat, *Rousettus lanosus*
Egyptian Fruit Bats, *Rousettus aegyptiacus*

Stenonycteris lanosus
Epomorphus anurus
Epomorphus minor labiatus

Family Rhinolophidae
Ruppell's Horseshoe Bat, *Rhinolophus furnigatus*
Rwenzori Horseshoe Bat, *Rhinolophus rwenzorii*
Arabian Horseshoe Bat, *Rhinolophus clivosus*

Family Megadermatidae
Yellow-winged Bat, *Lavia frons*

Family Molossidae
Little Free-tailed Bat, *Chaerophon pumila*
Angolan Free-tailed Bat, *Mops condylurus*
Dwarf Free-Tailed Bat, *Mops nanulus*
Martienssen's Free-Tailed Bat, *Otomops martiensseni*

Family Nycteridae
Egyptian Slit-Faced Bat, *Nycteris thebaica*

Family Vespertilionidae
White-winged Serotine, *Eptesicus tenuipinnis*
Moleney's Flat-headed Bat, *Mimetillus moloneyi*
Greater Long-fingered Bat, *Mimetillus inflatus*
Common Long-fingered Bat, *Miniopterus schriebersi*
Banana Bat, *Pipistrellus nanus*
African Giant House Bat, *Scotophilus nigrita*

Family Lorisidae (Bushbabies)
Dwarf Bushbaby, *Galago demidovii*
Senegal Galago, *Galago senegalensis*

Mammal List

Thomas' Galago, *Galago thomasi*
Bosman's Potto, *Peridictcus potto*

Family Cercopithecidae (Monkeys, Baboons)
White-nosed Monkey, *Cercopithecus ascanius*
L'Hoesti Monkey, *Cercopithecus l'hoesti*
Golden Monkey, *Cercopithecus mitis*
Black & White Colobus, *Colobus guereza*
Olive Baboon, *Papio anubis*

Family Pongidae (Great Apes)
Mountain gorilla, *Berengei berengei*
Common Chimpanzee, *Pan troglodytes*

Family Leporidae
Savanna (Crawshay's) Hare, *Lepus crawshayi*

Family Anomaluridae (Squirrels)
Lord Derby's Flying Squirrel, *Anomalurus derbianus*

Family Scuiridae (Squirrels)
Carruther's Mountain Tree Squirrel, *Funisciurus carruthersi*
Curvier's Fire-footed Squirrel, *Funisciurus pyrrhopus*
Red-legged Sun Squirrel, *Heliosciurus rufobrachium*
Montane Sun Squirrel, *Heliosciurus ruwenzorrii*
Alexander's Bush Squirrel, *Paraxerus alexandri*
Boehm's Bush Squirrel, *Paraxerus boehmi*
Giant Forest Squirrel, *Protoxerus strangeri*

Family Cricetidae (Rats and Mice)
Savanna Pouched Rat, *Cricetomys emini*
Forest Pouched Rat, *Cricetomys gambianus*

Rwenzori Climbing Mouse, *Dendromus kahuziensis*
African Climbing Mouse, *Dendromus mesomelas*
Western Climbling Mouse, *Dendromus messorius*
Chestnut Climbing Mouse, *Dendromus mystacalis*
Montane Groove-toothed Rat, *Otomys denti*
Tropical Groove-toothed Rat, *Otomys tropicalis*
Common Vlei Rat, *Otomys irroratus*
Northern Groove-toothed Rat, *Otomys typus*

Family Rhizomyidae
Mole Rat, *Tachyorystes splendens*

Family Thryonomyidae
Lesser Savanna Cane Rat, *Thryonomys gregorians*

Family Muridae (Rats and Mice)
Kaiser's Bush Rat, *Aethomys kaiseri*
Velvet Rat, *Colomys goslingi*
Shaggy Marsh Rat, *Dasymys incomptus*
Montane Marsh Rat, *Dasymys montanus*
Common Thicket Rat, *Grammomys dolichurus*
East African Montane Wood Mouse, *Hylomyscus denniae*
Common Striped Grass Mouse, *Lemniscomys striatus*
Eastern Brush-furred Rat, *Lophuromys flavopunctatus*
Yellow-Bellied Brush-Furred Rat, *Lophuromys luteogaster*
Medium-Tailed Brush-Furred Rat, *Lophuromys medicaudataus*
Rahm's Brush-Furred Rat, *Lophuromys rahmi*
Common Brush-furred Rat, *Lophuromys sikapusi*
Woosnam's Brush-furred Rat, *Lophuromys woosnami*
Northern Savanna Rat, *Mastomys hildebrandtii*
Western Rift Pygmy Mouse, *Mus bufo*
Pygmy Mouse, *Mus minutoides*

Mammal List

Tree-toed Grass Rat, *Mylomys dybowski*
Rusty-nosed Rat, *Oenomys hypoxanthus*
Common Creek Rat, *Pelomys fallax*
Papyrus Rat, *Pelomys hopkinsi*
Multimammate mouse, *Praomys denniae*
Jackson's Soft-furred , *Praomys jacksoni*
Black Rat, *Rattus rattus*
Montane Forest Rat, *Thammomys venustus*
Kemp's Forest Rat, *Thammomys kempi*
African Common Dormouse, *Graphiurus murinus*
Nile Grass Rat, *Arvicanthis niloticus*
East African Montane Wood Mouse, *Mylomyscus denniae*
Stella Wood Mouse, *Mylomyscus stella*

Family Gerbillidae
Northern Savanna Gerbil, *Tatera valida*

Family Hystricidae
Brush-tailed Porcupine, *Atherurus africanus*
South African Porcupine, *Hystrix africae-australis*

Family Canidae
Side-striped Jackal, *Canis adustus*

Family Felidae
African Golden Cat, *Felis aurata*
Serval, *Felis serval*
African Wild Cat, *Felis silvestris*
Serval, *Leptailurus serval*
Leopard, *Panthera pardus*

Family Mustelidae

Zorilla (Striped Polecat), *Ictonyx striatus*
Honey Badger, *Mellivora capensis*
East African Striped Weasel, *Poecilogale albinucha*

Family Viverridae
East African Civet, *Civettictis civetta*
Servaline Genet, *Genetta servalina*
Rusty Spotted Genet, *Genetta tigrina*
African Palm Civet, *Nandinia binotate*
African Civette, *Viverra civetta*

Family Herpestidae
Marsh Mongoose, *Atilax paludinosus*
Egyptian Mongoose, *Herpestes ichneumon*
Slender Mongoose, *Herpestes sanguineus*
White-tailed Mongoose, *Ichneumia abicaudata*
Banded Mongoose, *Mungos mungo*

Family Hyaenidae
Spotted Hyena, *Crocuta crocuta*

Family Manidae
Tree Pangolin, *Manis tricuspis*

Family Bovidae
Bongo, *Boocerus euryceros*
Bushbuck, *Tragelaphus scriptus*
Peter's Duiker, *Cephalophus callipygus*
White-bellied Duiker, *Cephalophus lecogaster*
Blue Duiker, *Cephalophus monticola*
Black-fronted Duiker, *Cephalophus nigrifrons*
Yellow-backed Duiker, *Cephalophus sylvicultor*

Mammal List

Forest Buffalo, *Syncerus caffer nanus*

Family Orycteropodidae
Aardvard (Ant Bear), *Orycteropus afer*

Family Elephantidae
African Forest Elephant, *Loxodonta africana*

Family Suidae
Giant Forest Hog, *Hylochoerus meinertzhageni*
White-faced Bushpig, *Potamochoerus lavatus hassama*
Red River Hog, *Potamochoerus porcus*

Family Procaviidae
Southern Tree Hyrax, *Dendrohydrax arboreus*

Volcanoes National Park Reptile and Amphibian List

Data Compiled by the Karisoke Research Center

Reptiles
Family Viperidae
Nitshe's Bush Viper, *Atheris nitschei*
Rhinoceros-Horned Viper, *Bitis nasicornis*

Family Chamaeleontidae
Elliot's Chameleon, *Chamaeleo ellioti*
Johnston's Chameleon or Three-Horned Chameleon, *Chamaeleo johnstoni*
Coarse Chameleon, *Chamaeleo rudis*
Striped Chameleon, *Chamaeleo bitaeniatus*
Flap-Neck Chameleon, *Chamaeleo dilepis*
Boulenger's Pygmy Chameleon, *Rhampholeon boulengeri*

Family Boiginae
Gunther's Green Tree Snake, *Dipsadoboa unicolor*

Family Colubrinae
Rwanda Forest Green Snake, *Philothamnus ruandae*
Large-eyed green treesnake, *Thrasops aethiopissa*
Forest Vine Snake, *Thelotornis kirtlandi*

Family Dasypeltinae
Montane Egg-eater, *Dasypeltis atra*
Angola Green Snake, *Philothamnus angolensis*

Family Lacertidae
Sparse-Scaled Forest Lizard, *Adolfus vaureselli*

Family Scincidae
Rwanda Five-Toed Skink, *Leptosiaphos graueri*
Grass Top Skink, *Mabuya megalura*
Virunga Four-Toed Skink, *Leptosiaphos hackarsi*

Family Geckkonidae
Four-Lined Forest Gecko, *Cnemaspis quattuorseriatus*

Amphibians
Family Pipidae
Montane Reed Frog, *Hyperolius casteneus*
Pitman's Common Reed Frog, *Hyperolius viridiflavus*

Family Bufonidae
Common River Frog, *Bufo angolensis*
Montane Golden Toad, *Bufo kisolensis*

Family Hyperoliidae
Karissimbi Forest Treefrog, *Leptopelis karissimbensis*
Warty Stripe-Legged Frog, *Phylyctimantis verrucosus*
De Witte's Clawed Frog, *Xenopus wittei*

Family Ranidae
Rana modestus
Cap River Frog, *Rana fuscigula*
Bayon's Common Reed Frog, *Rana viridiflavus*
Giant Torrent Frog, *Phrynobatrachus asper*

Index

11, Group, 46, 89, 111, 112
13, Group, 4, 98, 112
Acacia, 184
Africa, German East, 15
agriculture, 42, 49, 80, 120, 122, 140, 152, 157, 158, 199
AIDS, 51, 52
Airport, Kigali, 49, 86
Akeley, Carl, 9, 13, 179
Albert, Lake, 40
Alpine, 44, 124, 215
America, North, 42
America, South, 41
amphibians, 10, 167, 168, 170
Annee, Bonne, 73, 74, 79, 87
antelope, roan, 184
anthropology, 42
Ape, Great, 20, 192, 203, 204, 205, 208, 222
Appendix, 2, 5, 82, 125, 128, 138, 140, 142, 143, 160, 161, 167, 168
archaeological, 42
Army, Congolese, 187, 190
art, 57
babies, 97
bamboo, 104, 122, 123, 124, 133, 141, 143, 160, 163
Bank, World, 19
barks, 102
bats, 160, 220
beat, chest, 101
Bee-eater, 145, 215
beer, banana, 51, 55, 183
Beethoven, 84, 116
Belgian, King of, 13

Beringe, Captain Robert von, 9
Beringei, Gorilla, 12, 92, 93
beringei, Gorilla beringei, 12, 92
Berlin, Zoological Museum in, 12
Beston, Henry, 5, 89
bicycles, 28
Biodiversity, 205, 206
Bird List, 211
Birds of Volcanoes National Park, 143
birdwatchers, 142, 155
Bisoke, Mount, 38, 40, 45, 182
blackback, 84, 112
Blair, Tony, 9
Bongo, 225
Bono, 9
books, 9, 17, 28, 29, 35, 45, 50, 52, 60, 157
breeding, 97
buffalo, 226
buffalo, forest, 38, 155, 156, 158, 159
Bulera, Lake, 39, 171, 182
Burundi, 12, 15, 40, 140, 142, 164, 185, 206
Bush, George W., 9
Bush, Laura, 9, 52, 204
bushbuck, 155, 156, 157
Butare, 60, 178
Butterfly, African giant swallowtail, 172, 173
Café, Internet, 29, 63
Cambridge, 68, 86, 87, 205
camera, 36
Cameroon, 93
Camp, Karisoke Research, 46, 64, 124, 130, 178
Campbell, Bob, 69, 86, 130

cancer, 125
Cantsbee, 83
Canyon, Grand, 14
Carr, Rosamond, 2, 64, 70, 88, 204
Carr, Roz, 49, 86
cat, African golden, 163
celery, 104, 137
Census, 202
chameleon, 155, 167, 169
Channel, Discovery, 112, 198
Charlie, 75, 76, 77, 78, 79, 202, 203
checklist, 36
Chidester, Judy, 1, 65, 73, 74, 76
children, 11, 29, 33, 36, 52, 53, 54, 55, 60, 70
Chimpanzee, 10, 12, 21
Chronology, Dian Fossey, 85
Church, Ntarama, 49
Cindy, 65, 69, 75
cistern, 43
City, New York, 13, 121
Clinic, Bisate, 43
Clinton, Bill, 9, 51
Club, Rotary, 52
Coco, 69, 86, 87, 130, 174
Collins, Hotel Milles, 27
Congo, Belgian, 13, 15
Congo, Democratic Republic of, 5, 10, 16, 20, 22, 27, 62, 67, 85, 92, 109, 191, 193, 194, 202
Congo, Republic of, 5, 10, 16, 19, 20, 22, 27, 62, 67, 85, 92, 93, 109, 191, 193, 194, 202
conservation, 1, 17, 19, 20, 21, 40, 42, 58, 70, 80, 81, 92, 93, 109, 122, 140, 185, 188, 189, 190, 193, 195, 196, 199, 201, 204, 205, 206, 207, 208, 209
Conservation, Congo Institute for Nature, 81

Conservation, Partners in, 196
Crane, crowned, 66, 138, 139
Credits, Photo, 2
crest, sagittal, 95
crow, 152, 219
culture, 15, 27, 50, 57
currency, 18, 109
cypress, 42, 128
dancers, Itore, 55
deihli, Gorilla gorilla, 93
DFGFI, 1, 43, 44, 57, 58, 60, 64, 79, 80, 81, 82, 83, 92, 99, 107, 109, 110, 115, 118, 122, 127, 139, 142, 160, 178, 190, 192, 196, 198, 199
Dian Fossey Gorilla Fund, 1, 2, 4, 18, 52, 64, 79, 122, 139, 160, 192, 195, 202, 203,
diarrhea, 31, 75, 77
Digit, 17, 65, 82, 86, 87, 179
discovery, the, 11
disease, 21, 30, 97, 107, 198
diseases, zoonotic, 193, 197
District, Kisoro, 47
duiker, 225
Eagle, 212, 214
Ebola, 21, 90, 93
economy, 1, 160
Ecosystem, Virunga, 80, 121, 157, 159, 167, 174, 186, 188, 193, 194
ecotourism, 1, 4, 19, 52, 81, 160, 184, 189, 192, 196, 199
education, 52, 59, 175, 199
Edward, Lake, 40, 47, 192
Eland, Cape, 184
elephant, 226
Elizabeth, Queen, 13, 47, 155, 178
Embassy, 64, 71, 72, 74
endangered, 199, 204, 205
endangered, critically, 93

English, 29, 31, 60, 62, 81, 89, 111, 129, 142, 183
epidemic, respiratory, 197
eucalyptus, 42, 104, 128, 129, 167
exchange, foreign, 192
expressions, 61, 102
Fawcett, Katie, 1, 178, 186
fees, 159, 160, 196
fence, perimeter, 38
festivals, 62
Field Notes, 110, 116
Film, Lost, 69, 204
fish, 61, 171, 184
Five, Group, 82, 84, 112, 116
flatworm, 174
flies, 62, 173
flights, 62
flowers, 129, 135
fly, tsetse, 173
folklore, 57
food, 30, 61, 77, 97, 100, 103, 104, 112, 120, 126, 128, 131, 132, 133, 134, 135, 137, 152, 159, 162, 164, 197, 199
forest, 1, 43, 95, 122, 140, 145, 162, 185, 201, 202, 220, 222, 224, 226, 227
Forest, Gishwati, 160
Forest, Nyungwe, 160
Fossey, Dian, 1, 2, 4, 5, 8, 9, 17, 18, 27, 40, 44, 52, 64, 66, 68, 69, 71, 72, 77, 79, 80, 85, 103, 111, 112, 115, 116, 122, 124, 130, 139, 160, 174, 175, 177, 179, 181, 183, 192, 195, 201, 202, 203, 204, 205, 206, 208
Foundation, African Wildlife, 43, 190, 201
Francolin, 144, 145, 213
French, 29, 31, 60, 61, 81, 111, 142, 183
French-English, 29, 60
frogs, 168, 170

future, 203
galagos, 184
Gallium, 104, 125
Genocide, 50, 51, 62, 205
Geologists, 40, 41, 44
geology, 39
Geology of Volcanoes National Park, 39
gestation, 97
gifts, 60
giraffe, 157, 158, 184
giant lobelia, 48, 134
goat, 61
Goodall, Alan, 2, 64, 86
Goodall, Jane, 69
Gorilla, Cross River, 21, 93
gorilla, Gorilla gorilla, 93
gorillas, orphaned, 192
GRASP, 192, 208
Group, Agashya, 112
Group, Amahoro, 112
Group, Hirwa, 112
Group, Kwitonda, 112
Group, Rugendo, 189
Group, Sabyinyo, 4, 8, 34, 56, 98, 112, 175, 198
Group, Susa, 32, 56, 107, 112
Group, Umbano, 112
groups, gorilla, 82
groups, habituated, 46, 109, 111, 189
grubs, 174
Guhonda, 8, 56, 95, 98, 112, 198
Guide, 1, 18, 32, 56, 201
Guineo-Congolian, 40
Habyarimana, 178
Hagenia, 64, 120, 122, 124, 125, 126, 129, 130, 131, 141, 143, 144, 145, 147, 148, 149, 150, 151, 152, 164, 176, 179, 180
Heritage, World, 19, 21, 22, 189
hierarchy, 95

231

INDEX

Highlands, Kigezi (Rukigi), 19
hiking, 26, 182
Hills, Land of a Thousand, 2, 49, 70, 204
history, 13, 14, 15, 65
History, American Museum of Natural, 13, 14, 15
hog, giant forest, 156, 164
hog, Red River, 164
holidays, 62
homes, 33, 53, 56, 194
hoots, 100
Hotel, Novotel, 27
Hutu, 15, 52, 57, 194
hyena, spotted, 163
Hypericum, 105, 121, 122, 124, 125, 126, 131, 144, 147, 149, 150
hyrax, 226
I, World War, 15
II, World War, 15
illiteracy, 52, 53, 54
IMAX, 12, 48, 178, 205
impala, 184
infant, 117
infanticide, 97
insects, 160, 164, 167, 171, 172, 173
interactions, 98, 107, 112
Internet, 29, 37, 43, 50, 62, 80, 81
invertebrates, 104, 167, 174
Irwin, Steve, 68
IUCN, 19, 21, 93, 140, 141, 163, 170, 189, 205
Izina, Kwita, 18
jacket, 36, 56
juveniles, 35, 97, 101
Kagame, Paul, 1, 52, 58, 59, 112, 206
Karisimbi, Mount, 40, 44, 45, 46, 121, 182
Karisoke Research Center, 1, 4, 18, 52, 54, 79, 82, 103, 127, 142, 157, 161, 175, 178, 186, 199, 203, 227

Kenya, 27, 40, 49, 57, 62, 89, 142, 155, 206
Kigali, 18, 27, 28, 30, 37, 49, 51, 52, 57, 61, 62, 64, 71, 72, 74, 76, 86, 138, 178, 182, 183
Kima, 65, 162
King, Tutsi, 15
Kingdom, Belgian, 14
Kingdom, Wild, 84, 87
Kinigi, 4, 26, 27, 29, 31, 32, 42, 52, 128, 152, 182
Kinshasa, 20, 193
Kinyarwanda, 29, 45, 61, 110
Kivu, Lake, 40, 70, 161, 171
Kivu, North, 192
Kurira, 56, 112
Lakes, Great, 39, 171, 190
Land of a Thousand Hills, 2, 49, 70, 204
Land of the Mountain Gorilla, 9
languages, 60
laughs, 101
lava, 42
Leakey, 67
leopard, 163, 224
Leopold, Albert, 13
Life, My, 51, 202
Lilly, Alecia, 1, 92
Lily, 70, 175
list, mammal, 220
Lobelia, 104, 121, 125, 126, 134, 135
Lobelia, giant, 48, 134
Lodge, Akagera Game, 184
Lodge, Gorillas Nest, 182, 210
lunch, 30
Madagascar, 42, 169, 214
Magazine, National Geographic, 86
Magazine, Time, 13, 203
malaria, 173
Mammals of Volcanoes National Park, 156, 161

mammoths, woolly, 42
Mara, Masai, 49, 155
Massif, Mitumba, 40
Meadow, Alpine, 44
Meadow, Kabara, 15, 16, 67, 82, 86, 152, 164, 179
measles, 198
medicine, 31
Memorial, Genocide, 50, 62
Memorial, Gisozi, 52
Memorial, Murambi, 51
Merode, Emmanuel de, 190
MGVP, 196, 197, 198
Mikeno, Mount, 40
Mikeno, Old Man of, 13
Mist, Gorillas in the, 1, 17, 67, 69, 82, 83, 84, 87, 88, 111, 112, 116, 179, 183, 203, 204
monkey, blue, 162
monkeys, black-faced vervet, 184
monkeys, colobus, 184
monkeys, golden, 160, 182
monkeys, owl-faced, 185
Moon, Mountains of the, 40
Mountains, Ruwenzori, 40, 47
Mowat, Farley, 69
Mugisha, Lake, 39
Muhabura, Hotel, 4, 27, 28, 30, 182
Muhavura, Mount, 47, 182
Musanze, 54
music, 57
musicians, 57
naming, 109, 111, 182
National Geographic, 2, 8, 17, 67, 69, 84, 86, 87, 130, 190, 201, 204, 206
Nations, League of, 15
Nichols, Michael, 17, 206
Nigeria, 93
Nile, 40, 224

Nkunda, Laurent, 191
notes, 110, 116, 128, 130, 131, 132, 134, 135, 136, 137, 143, 144, 145, 146, 147, 148, 149, 150, 151, 152, 161, 162, 163, 164, 165
Nyakagezi, 46, 48
Nyiramachabelli, 64, 179
okapi, 158
Omaha, Mutual of, 84
Organization, Gorilla, 81, 208
Organizations, Gorilla Conservation, 208
organizations, non-profit, 160, 195, 196
orientation, 31, 33
Orphanage, Imbabazi, 70
ORTPN (RDB), 1, 18, 31, 33, 36, 37, 43, 44, 46, 52, 60, 81, 109, 111, 112, 115, 122, 140, 142, 155, 160, 180, 182, 185, 186, 196, 210
Other Animals of Volcanoes National Park, 168
Pablo, 82, 107, 110, 112, 116, 118, 119, 179
Pangaea, 42
parasites, 82, 198
Park, Akagera National, 27, 40, 141, 155, 178, 183, 184, 207
Park, Albert National, 14, 15, 88, 179
Park, Big Bend National, 138
Park, Bwindi Impenetrable National, 19, 92, 104, 107, 122, 188
Park, Kahuzi-Biega National, 92
Park, Kibira National, 185
Park, Mahinga Gorilla National, 10, 41
Park, Maiko National, 93
Park, Nyungwe National, 141, 178, 184, 185
Park, Queen Elizabeth, 47, 155, 178
Park, Virunga National, 10, 16, 19, 22, 27, 38, 81, 157, 158, 159, 169, 171, 172, 186, 187, 189, 190, 195, 207, 209

233

INDEX

Park, Yellowstone National, 12
Parks, Office of Rwanda Tourism and National, 18
Party, Parmehutu, 15
People of Rwanda, 50
permits, 37
photo, satellite, 44
photography, 36
photography, flash, 35
pig, white-faced bush, 164
Planning Your Trip, 26
Plants of Volcanoes National Park, 121, 125, 128
Pleistocene, 40, 41, 42, 203
Pliocene, 41
poaching, 72
pollution, 62
potto, 161, 222
poverty, 11, 56, 194
Precambrian, 41
Program, International Gorilla Conservation, 109, 122, 140, 188, 190, 195, 204, 208, 209
Program, Partners in Conservation, 58
Programs, socio-economic, 160
Project, Great Apes Survival, 192, 208
projects, community, 17, 18
Puck, 83, 84, 110, 118
Pucker, 69, 86, 87, 130, 174
Pyrethrum, 18, 137
Queen Elizabeth, 13, 47, 155, 178
radio, 57, 202
Rafiki, 84
raven, 152, 219
rehabilitate, 19, 192
religion, 61
Reptile and Amphibian List, 227
reptiles, 10, 142, 167, 168, 169

RDB, 1, 18, 31, 33, 36, 37, 43, 44, 46, 52, 60, 81, 109, 111, 112, 115, 122, 140, 142, 155, 160, 180, 182, 185, 186, 196, 210
rescue, 192
research, 1, 4, 18, 46, 52, 54, 64, 72, 79, 82, 103, 112, 115, 124, 127, 130, 142, 156, 161, 167, 175, 178, 186, 199, 203, 211, 220, 227
Reserve, Tayna Nature, 192
rest, 106
restrooms, 29
Rhuengerhi (Musanze), 4, 18, 79
Richardson, Clare, 1
ridge, brow, 94
Rift, 40, 125, 141, 171, 172, 199, 205, 207, 223
Rift, Albertine, 40, 125, 141, 171, 172, 199, 205, 207
river, 21, 40, 76, 93, 112, 164, 184, 203, 226, 227
roads, 29
Rotary, 52
Rubavu, 2, 54, 70, 71, 161, 162, 183
Ruhondo, Lake, 20, 39, 182
Ruwenzori, 40, 47, 218
Rwanda, Hotel, 27
Safaris, Volcanoes, 27
Schaller, George, 9, 15, 44, 67, 103, 129, 179
school, 43, 85
screams, 100
security, 62, 195
Sembagare, 70
Senecio, 125, 132
Senkekwe, 82
serval, 163, 224
Service, United States Forest, 43
Service, US Fish and Wildlife, 192, 196, 199

shrew, 220
sickness, sleeping, 173
silverback, 77, 94, 119, 129
sleet, 44
snails, 171, 172
snakes, 168, 169, 170
snares, 56
soccer, 58
Society, Wildlife Conservation, 17, 93, 122, 139, 205, 207, 208, 209
soldiers, 85
sports, 58
Stilgar, 89, 111
stores, grocery, 30
Strait, Bering, 42
stratovolcano, 44
Subalpine, 124, 132, 143, 144, 147, 148, 149, 150, 151, 163
sunbird, 141, 150, 218
Swahili, 45
swamp, 140, 220
system, classification, 15
Tanganyika, Lake, 39, 40, 171
Tanzania, 40, 142, 155, 184, 205, 206
taxi, 29, 51
taxonomists, 92
technology, 60
termites, 171, 174
thistle, 135
threats, 19, 91, 94, 192, 205
Tiger, 65, 85
Tilapia, 171
Times, New, 50, 52, 205
Titus, 84, 116
toilet, 36
topi, 183
tourism, 17, 18, 37, 71, 111, 204, 210
tourism, gorilla, 17, 18, 29, 111
trackers, 29, 31, 182

traditions, 57
transfer, 116, 117, 119
trek, 30, 33, 36
Tshahafi, Lake, 39
Turaco, 139, 141, 144, 214
turtles, 169, 196
Tutsi, 15, 57
TV, National Geographic, 17
Twa, 15, 57, 86
Uganda, 5, 10, 19, 22, 39, 40, 41, 46, 47, 48, 62, 92, 95, 104, 108, 109, 110, 122, 140, 142, 155, 159, 178, 182, 189, 199, 202, 204, 206
UN, 191
UNESCO, 21, 53, 57, 163, 189, 202, 207
United Nations, 2, 9, 15, 19, 20, 21, 53, 59, 194, 195
university, 15, 60, 68, 73, 80, 84, 86, 87, 201, 203, 205, 206
University, Cornell, 73, 84, 87
Urundi, 15
Valley, Great Rift, 40
Valley, Rift, 40
Veit, Peter, 77
venomous, 170
Vernonia, 105, 127, 132
veterinary, 56, 112, 192, 196
Victoria, Lake, 39, 61
Viper, 169
vocalizations, 99
Volcano, Nyamuragira, 38, 40, 41, 49
Volcano, Nyriagongo, 27
Volcano, Sabyinyo, 11, 14, 27
Volcans, Parc National des, 10
War, Civil, 52, 85, 178
warming, global, 199
weather, 37
Weaver, Sigourney, 17, 83
wildlifedirect.org, 81, 186, 195, 208

235

INDEX

worms, 174
Yosemite, 14
Zaire, 67, 89
Ziz, 119

Zoo, Albuquerque, 94
Zoo, Antwerp, 93
Zoo, Cologne, 69, 86, 87
Zoo, Columbus, 58, 196

Photo Credits

All images copyright of the photographer

Rick LoBello cover

Rick LoBello inside cover to page 4

National Geographic Society pages 6-7

Rick LoBello page 8

Alex Buchanan page 10

Lucy Mayer page 14

Alessandra Magni page 16

Gerald Cloud page 18

Samantha Lloyd pages 20, 23

Rick LoBello page 24

Martin Lustyk page 26

Darren Kumasawa page 28, 32

Rick LoBello page 34, 38

Donna Sevilla page 39

Brandon Thiessen page 41

Martin Lustyk page 45

Marcell Claassen page 47

Stefan Westerheide page 48

UN/DPI Photo page 50

Stefan Westerheide page 53

Tavis Beaubier page 54

Samantha Lloyd page 55

Photo Credits

Rick LoBello page 58

UN/DPI Photo by Paulo Filgueiras page 59

Stefan Westerheide page 63, 66

Dr. Alan Goodall pages 68, 71, 73

Rick LoBello page 74

Elizabeth Escher page 76

Judy Chidester page 79

Rick LoBello page 83

Gerald Cloud page 91

Brandon Thiessen page 92

Rick LoBello page 94

Emile Ige page 96

Rick LoBello pages 98, 103, 105, 106, 108,

Dr. Alan Goodall pages 117, 119

Samantha Lloyd page 120

Jon Clark page 121

Rick LoBello page 123

Gerald Cloud page 124

Alessandra Magni page 129

Dr. Alan Goodall pages 130, 131

Samantha Lloyd page 133

Stefan Westerheide page 134

Rick LoBello page 136, 139

Dr. Alan Goodall page 144

Samantha Lloyd page 146

Jonas Van de Voorde pages 151

Rick LoBello page 153

Jonas Van de Voorde pages 154

Lee Braverman page 156

Dr. Alan Goodall page 158

Marcus Richardson page 162

Rick LoBello page 165

Dr. Alan Goodall page 166

Rick LoBello page 167

Samatha Lloyd pages 168, 172

Robert Nash page 173

Samatha Lloyd pages 176, 177, 180, 181, 183

Emile Ige page 185

Innocent Mburanumwevia page 187

Rob Verhoeven page 188

UN/DPI Photo by Marie Frechon page 191, 193

UN/DPI Photo by Ryan Brown page 195

Rob Verhoeven page 197

Gerald Cloud page 210